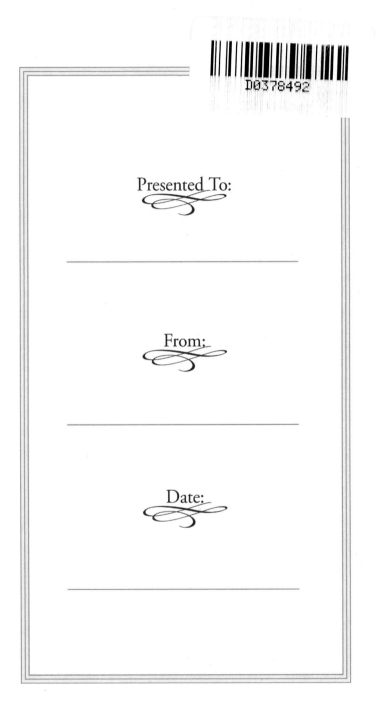

Presented To:

_____

From:

_____

Date:

_____

POWER

POWER

TO
CHANGE
YOUR WORLD

DANNY MCDANIEL

DESTINY IMAGE₍ₑ₎ PUBLISHERS, INC.
P.O. Box 310, Shippensburg, PA 17257-0310
"Promoting Inspired Lives."

This book and all other Destiny Image, Revival Press, Mercy-Place, Fresh Bread, Destiny Image Fiction, and Treasure House books are available at Christian bookstores and distributors worldwide.

For a U.S. bookstore nearest you, call 1-800-722-6774.
For more information on foreign distributors, call 717-532-3040.
Reach us on the Internet: www.destinyimage.com.

ISBN 13 TP: 978-0-7684-0282-7
ISBN 13 Ebook: 978-0-7684-8807-4

For Worldwide Distribution, Printed in the U.S.A.
1 2 3 4 5 6 7 8 / 16 15 14 13 12

DEDICATION

I dedicate this book to my sons, Cam, Gavin, and TJ, who have been consecrated to the Lord to preach the gospel to the ends of the earth.

ACKNOWLEDGMENTS

I am grateful for…

My wife, Diane, for her patience and grace. She truly is the love of my life.

My dad, Mac, who prayed for me diligently for 13 years to come back to the Lord.

Pastor Joe Saucido from El Paso, TX for giving me the little pink book that changed my life and led to me being "set free" by the Holy Spirit.

Randall and Pat Jones from Round Rock, TX, for ministering freedom to me, and laying hands on me to receive the promise of the Holy Spirit.

Ronnie and Brenda Chance from Kingwood, TX, for praying for me and for bringing necessary wisdom and knowledge to my attention at the right time in my life.

All of our friends who have chosen to "Only Believe!", and receive the promise of the Holy Spirit in order to be equipped to fulfill their destiny on this earth.

My sons, who have chosen to walk as true sons of Abraham, Isaac, Jacob, and of the most High God.

CONTENTS

PREFACE

We live in a world that is so captivated by power. Whether it is in the business world, athletics, or the world of entertainment, displays of power are what seem to be most attractive to the masses. People are racing to the movie theaters when the next great superhero movie is released. People are drawn to the television to watch the most dominating sports team of the day. And people are consistently attracted to stories from any source of media concerning the rich and the famous. I have to admit that just a few days ago I took my two younger sons into the Trump Tower in New York City, and we had our picture taken with Donald Trump as he autographed his book for us! Doing that is not normal for me because I teach and train in the business world about how not to put people on pedestals. Yet, there was something very alluring about walking into the Trump Tower and getting to meet Donald Trump.

THERE MUST BE MORE

The mystery in all of this is that if God created the heavens and the earth, and if Jesus conquered the devil and holds the keys to death and hell, where is all the power? Why aren't people flocking to the church instead of the movie theater? Why aren't people glued to watching Christian television for hours on end? Why aren't people buying tickets to get into an arena of 75,000 people to hear the powerful evangelist preach God's word, see blind eyes open, the lame walk, and the sick healed? Why do more people know who Donald Trump is than know who Reinhard Bonnke is?

When I got saved in 1998, I was full of joy and excitement over my new commitment to live for Christ. But something deep down inside of me knew there had to be more. I knew that if I was going to give my life over to Jesus, then He must have a more exciting plan for me than all of the things the world had to offer. I knew God had so much more to offer me than what I had seen in just a few days as a Christian. So the quest began.

My wife and I both embarked on a journey of prayer, Bible studies, and crying out to the Lord for "all" He had to offer us as Christians while we still lived on this earth. Our prayers were persistent as we cried out to Him to show us more, to reveal Himself to us in ways we did not know. We also had an open heart and were willing to explore any area of spiritual growth that we could obtain, while praying for God's protection to guard us from deception. As always, He was faithful and He answered our cries. Those answers are what this book is all about.

God wants us to live our life on this earth as models for Him. We cannot be effective disciples without power. Even Jesus had to have power while He walked on this earth, and it was Him who told us that we had to have power from on high (see Luke 24:49). So that means we need to find out how to obtain this power He spoke of. We know the power only comes from God, but He wants you to have it. He wants you to be entrusted with it so that you can be an ambassador for Him on this earth.

WHY I WROTE THIS BOOK

I wrote this book out of obedience to God's promptings in my life. It has been written in order for you to become a highly effective agent for change in the world today. It is important that the reader know that, like any book outside of the Bible, this is *not* the Bible! This is a book that is intended to help you see God's word the way He wants you to see it, and obtain the power to walk out all He has commanded for you to do.

At the time that this book is being written, I am a church planter, a pastor, and a businessman. My wife and I are entrepreneurs and we have been immensely blessed in the business arena. However, it is important to note that this book is not an extension of any business endeavor that we are a part of. I work in the secular marketplace; therefore, my thoughts and opinions are not endorsed or associated with any business, corporation, or secular entity in the business world. I am writing this as a minister of God with the intent of touching the lives of millions of people around the world who want to live for God in such a way that causes change to occur all around them.

This book is challenging because it will cause you to dig deeper and decide if you really want to take God's word at face value. After all, His word is living and powerful, sharper than any two-edged sword (see Heb. 4:12). If this is the case, then His word is alive and must be taken at face value. In addition to this, it is designed to cut through every area of your life to get to the core of your heart and soul so that your spirit can divinely connect with His Spirit. It is the stuff in our heart and our soul that will fight "tooth and nail" to resist the cutting-edge truth of God's word. The writer of Hebrews said it this way: *"For the word of God is living and powerful, and sharper than any two-edged sword, piercing even to the division of soul and spirit, and of joints and marrow, and is a discerner of the thoughts and intents of the heart"* (Heb. 4:12).

As challenging as this book might be, it is packed with good news! It's all about perspective. I believe there is so much good news that follows within these pages that anyone who devours this book from cover to cover will have his or her life changed forever! It is quite possible that your prayers have been answered and God sent you this book so that He could show you how He wants to prepare you for greater things. God's answers to our prayers rarely show up in the exact shape, form, and size that we think they should. But His thoughts are so much higher than ours and His ways are not our ways (see Isa. 55:8-9). I am thankful that He used a wonderful man in El Paso, Texas, in December of 2000, to stick a little pink book in my hand that answered all of my prayers and led me to all of the things you are about to read.

And for you, the best is yet to come!

DANNY MCDANIEL

Chapter 1

WHY SHOULD WE STAY STUCK?

INITIAL QUESTIONS

This book has been written for the purpose of teaching you the word of God, as to how you can receive the promise of the Holy Spirit as described in the Gospels and in the Book of Acts. This book is not about your salvation. In general terms, what it takes to get to heaven is to be born again. However, if we are born again at the age of 9, 19, 39, or even 59, do we not have enough time left to experience all of that which God has for us here on earth? Should we not live a life that strives toward sanctification, to be set apart and made holy? Should we not, as God promises, be taken from glory to glory (see 2 Cor. 3:18)? Should we not believe that we don't know all the mysteries of the kingdom of God, and should we not want to live a life with an open heart so that we can receive all God has for us? Should we not expect to live a life filled with the power of God that makes a difference in the lives of other people? And should we not live a life that demonstrates more power than satan and all of his demonic forces are currently demonstrating on earth?

Or should we believe only what man has taught us? Should we live out our lives with a degree of stubbornness that is resistant to believe anything other than what our father taught us, our grandmother taught us, or our pastor taught us?

DOCTRINAL DIFFERENCES

I have seen multitudes of people over the years be so resistant to the things of God merely because they refuse to believe that their grandparents, their parents, or their pastor or priest could have been wrong all of these years. I firmly believe that we must live a life dedicated to believing what God says, and not base our doctrinal views on what man has convinced us over the years. I believe in the doctrines of Christ, and confidently believe that there are no others worth giving any credit to in order to establish the foundations for that which we should believe and live by.

When Paul visited the church in Corinth, as told in the first book of Corinthians, he addressed the church with a message of truth that applies to us even today. Paul had been hearing reports from his disciples in Corinth that there were contentions among people in the house of God. Because of this, he had to unwind their thinking and get them back on track and focused on Christ.

> *Now I say this, that each of you says, "I am of Paul," or "I am of Apollos," or "I am of Cephas," or "I am of Christ." Is Christ divided? Was Paul crucified for you? Or were you baptized in the name of Paul? I thank God that I baptized none of you except Crispus and Gaius, lest anyone should say that I had baptized in my own name* (1 Corinthians 1:12-15).

How does this relate to today? There is no doubt there are many doctrinal differences in the church of God (I am not referring to a particular denomination, but the church itself as Paul described), and these differences have caused contentions among Christians all across the world. There are Christians living next door to each other who won't talk to one another because they belong to a different denomination. There are local churches that will not co-labor together for the sake of reaching the lost in their communities because of doctrinal differences and contentions. There are Christian pastors who are living in the same communities and will have nothing to do with each other because of doctrinal differences and contentions.

I believe that if Paul were here today, his message would be quite the same: "Some of you say I am of the Baptists," or "I am of the Methodists," or "I am of the Church of Christ," or "I am of the Presbyterians," or "I am of the Assemblies of God," or "I am of the Charismatics," or "I am of one of the other 33,000-plus denominations out there today."

I believe Paul would go on to say, much like he continued to address the church at Corinth, "How can I teach anything new because of the divisions among you? How can I teach you anything that you will receive when you put more trust in those who have come before you than you put in God's word and what He is trying to show you?"

Paul goes on to validate his point in the 3rd chapter of First Corinthians:

And I, brethren, could not speak to you as to spiritual people but as to carnal, as to babes in Christ. I fed you with milk and not with solid food; for until now you were not able to receive it, and even now you are still not able; for you are still carnal. For where there are envy, strife, and divisions among you, are you not carnal and behaving like mere men? For when one says, "I am of Paul," and another, "I am of Apollos," are you not carnal? (1 Corinthians 3:1-4)

What a message for us today! Because we, the church of God, have the envy, strife, and divisions amongst each other, are we not still carnal? Are we limiting what God has for us, or what He wants to do through us? Are we not behaving like mere men? Are we more proud of our denominational status than we are belonging to Christ Jesus? Are we too proud of what we have been taught, and too proud of what we think we know as truth, to humble ourselves before God with an open heart and receive all He has promised us?

Or are we more focused on pleasing our grandma rather than God? Are we more focused on not disappointing our father than we are in pleasing the one true God? Are we more focused on adhering to the doctrines of man that we have been taught by our religious affiliations rather than opening up our heart to whatever God has stated in His word that is available to us? I believe it is time to get over our doctrinal differences and begin to take God at His word. There is no better time than now to get unstuck in our relationship with Him. Let me share some of my story with you.

Chapter 2

THE TRANSFORMATION

MY STORY OF TRANSFORMATION

I was 35 years old when I received what I am about to share with you in this book. I was mostly raised in Southern Baptist churches while growing up. I remember attending the Episcopal church as a young child because my mother was raised as an Episcopalian. My father was raised in Baptist and Pentecostal backgrounds, but he chose to take us to the Baptist church because of its dominant influence in the regions of West Texas. I was born again at the age of 10 and I was baptized the same night. When I left for college, however, I believe I only attended church one time over the next 13 years. Needless to say, I turned away from God and lived a life of total rebellion from the time I was 18 until I was 31.

I got married two years after graduating from college to my lovely wife, Diane, who was born and raised as a Roman Catholic, which was all she knew.

My wife and I started to attend a non-denominational church when I was about 30 years old simply because one of my coaching colleagues' best friends was the pastor. We were tired of struggling financially and never being able to overcome any of our circumstances. We had a very happy marriage, and had two young boys, but everything around us always seemed to fail—that is why I began to take my family back to church.

Church was somewhat of a struggle for us, being that Diane was a Catholic and I really didn't care—I just wanted answers. The importance of remaining Catholic was a big issue with Diane because she did not want to disappoint her family. Eventually, we were led to a Lutheran church in the Austin, Texas, area that had a contemporary service for the younger generation of Lutherans. The Lutheran church was a great balance for us, since it gave Diane some comfort in regards to the conservatism and some of the liturgy. More than that, it was right where God wanted us, to be able to draw us closer together and closer to Him.

About that time, in 1998, I met Jesus again at a Promise Keepers conference in the Houston Astrodome. It was a Friday night, and about 50,000 men were singing "Amazing Grace" when Jesus came into my life and flooded my heart as I sang that song. I was truly a new creature! I quit drinking beer and I quit using any form of profane words. In fact, all types of profane words became repulsive to me.

TWO LESSONS ABOUT PROFANITY

Some Christians have a tendency to stop using profanities when they are born again. However, they substitute their old vocabulary with what I call "Christian curse words." Christian curse words include words such as "dad gommit" and "freakin." I believe Christians need to wake up and clean up their mouths. God expects His people to be set apart and model Jesus to the world. I can't imagine Him being pleased with people who call themselves Christians, running around using "loose language" like this when there are so many other words one could choose.

In 2006, when our oldest son was in the 8th grade, we were riding in the car one day when I heard him use the word "freakin" as an adjective in reference to describing something—"That was freakin awesome!" When we got home, I pulled him and our middle child, who was in 5th grade, into our home office and used this event as a valuable learning experience. The first question I asked was, "Boys, how many words are there in the English language?"

Each replied, "I don't know." To be honest, I didn't either. But I did know enough to tell the boys that there were several hundred thousand words in the English language! The range of English words vary from 475,000 to over 900,000, depending on which dictionary you prefer.

I got out a dry erase marker and a board to write on, and the boys and I listed most of the common profanities known to them, in which they had heard many times during their school years. In another column, we listed all of the slang words and substitute curse words that people use in place of your average vulgar profanities.

There were two lessons that were to be learned from this. One was that most slang words contain very minimal changes that allow a so-called "Christian" to justify using a vulgar term by switching around a couple of letters. The apostle Paul wrote about this matter in Colossians when he stated, *"But now you yourselves are to put off all these: anger, wrath, malice, blasphemy, filthy language out of your mouth"* (Col. 3:8). I taught the boys about the motives behind "Christian slang" and "Christian curse words," and how the devil loves to try and deceive us. Satan knows that whether we say the "real" word or the slang term, in our heart we mean the same thing. The Bible warns us to not fall into traps due to the subtle tricks of satan and his devices (see 2 Cor. 2:11).

The second lesson learned from this was how few words there are in our English language that are deemed "unacceptable" compared to those which we can use. I asked our boys, "Out of all the hundreds of thousands of words in the English language, do you think we can restrain from using these twenty or so words? Is that too hard?"

They replied, "No, dad. It makes sense." My boys learned a valuable lesson from this incident. The apostle Paul instructed us in Second Timothy to purge ourselves from dishonor so we can become sanctified and useful for the Master, prepared for every good work (see 2 Tim. 2:21). We, as Christians, are to purge ourselves! When we do, we can become sanctified, which means to be set apart and made holy. When we become sanctified, we are useful to God and prepared to do good works and let our light shine before all men! This, of course, does not include filthy language or slang!

GOD'S LEADING AND GUIDANCE

The following Wednesday after the 1998 Promise Keepers event, I started my first men's Bible study that flourished for several years. It was at this time that Diane's family saw that their daughter was exploring other options and began to give me Catholic conversion tapes and books. I was so open to what God had for me that I would listen to every one of their tapes and read every one of their books. I will say that the Catholic conversion materials were quite interesting, and also very challenging. They challenged me to dig deeper for truth and to seek God for answers. I was not anti-Catholic because I knew little about the Catholic faith. But I was pro-God. I wanted what God wanted for my family and me, and I told Him that I trusted in Him for real truth. In fact, Diane and I agreed to pray to God that if He wanted us in the Catholic church, "then take us there," and if He wanted us in the Lutheran church, "then take us there." We tried both churches and we both had an open heart to obey God with His answer. Without a shadow of a doubt, He had us planted in this wonderful Lutheran church with a wonderful pastor who loved us and mentored us.

In January of 1999, we were flipping channels on television one late Sunday night, and we caught a young pastor speaking. I believe that it was his second sermon he preached after his father's death. We had never heard of his father, but we loved what he was preaching. As we waited anxiously every Sunday night for this young pastor to come on television, we began to sense that the Lord had more for us, but we knew it wasn't going to take place where we were. My pastor, whom I loved and respected deeply, asked me to be on the board of directors for the Lutheran church, but that was not what God had for our family.

We began praying, "Lord, do with us whatever Your will is for us. Take us to the spiritual home that we need to be to receive whatever it is You have for us." It wasn't long before He led us smack dab into the middle of a non-denominational church in Austin, Texas. As soon as we opened the front door of the church and walked in, Diane began to weep and shed tears. We knew that this was where God was leading us.

We were so blessed by sitting in this church for two years, and serving in the children's ministry. The teaching was just what God had for us during that season. Every time we went to church, we received from the Lord, and we grew as individuals and as a family.

It was during this time that the book *The Prayer of Jabez*, by Bruce Wilkinson, was hitting the market, and Diane and I had been praying fervently for God to "bless us indeed, and enlarge our territory, and lay His hand upon us, and guard us from evil, so that we would not cause Him pain" (see 1 Chron. 4:10). We both believed that there had to be more than what we were experiencing. The pastors we were listening to in church and on television at night were opening up our minds and our hearts to not have any limits as to what God wanted to do with our lives, or what He wanted to show us. What we found was that God always answers prayer, just not always in the form in which we think it ought to be answered. Sometimes, when we are not in tune with God, we can miss the very answer that He has for us in regards to our prayer. It was because of the prayer of Jabez that we realized that God has the right answer for our prayers, and we must be on the alert to recognize that which He has provided for us. Looking back, I can connect all the dots and can see how easily we could have missed God's answer to our prayers. Praise God we were so hungry that we were tuned in and on the alert!

Our answer to this prayer came on a business trip to El Paso, Texas, to work with a youth minister in order to help him build his new business. The first thing that the youth minister did was take me to his church to meet his father and the rest of the church leaders. His father gave me a tour of the church. While on the tour, I was intrigued because there was something different about these people—they were full of joy, and the light of God was all around them. What I saw caused me to ask questions. The pastor gave me a book that introduced what some would consider "deeper truths" from scripture. That book gave my wife and me some knowledge of God's power that led to some real spiritual breakthroughs in our lives.

Needless to say, that was our answer to our prayer—for God to expand our territory, for Him to uproot our fence posts (referring to the prayer of Jabez) and expand our boundaries. He had a work to do in us first. There were some areas of our past that had to get cleaned up before He could give us more. God changed my life and my family's life forever as a result of reading and responding to this book. It's funny how God opens new doors for us when we walk through the door that He is prompting us to walk through. Amazingly, each step that we take leads us to other doors that God has for us.

A POWERFUL SECOND EXPERIENCE

We were immediately led to an open door in the house of a wonderful couple in an outreach ministry from Round Rock, Texas. They were members and leaders of a prominent Baptist church in Round Rock. I didn't care about what denominational church they went to, I just cared about the truth. My wife and I were able to connect with this couple as a result of us having mutual friends who introduced us.

About five of us went over to this particular couple's house one night for a Bible teaching. We met this man, sat down, and he took us straight to the Book of Acts. He began to teach us for what seemed to be an hour about a second experience beyond salvation, that there was much more for us after we got saved. He began to lay out the principles that Jesus laid out to His disciples, and on which they acted upon. He continued to impress upon us that the word *upon* was a key word being used to describe a supernatural experience, or a supernatural power from on high, that was available to all believers after salvation.

I was 35 years old and I was hearing this for the very first time. Imagine the thoughts that run through your mind when you were raised in church for 18 years, you've been saved for five years, and have been chasing God with every ounce of energy that you have, and you are just now hearing about a second experience that is available to all who believe. You might be angry. You might be skeptical. You might be stubborn. Or you might be like me, who had the attitude of, "Praise God! Thank You, Lord! If there's more, then I want it!"

One of my friends who I took with me beat me to the punch. As soon as the minister was through teaching, my buddy was the first one to say, "I'm ready for whatever God has for me, so let's get this thing done!" This was the first time in my life that I can remember a man getting hands laid on him and the Holy Spirit coming upon him with power. I saw my friend, who was far from theatrical or comical, fall on the floor and lay there for what seemed to be 15 minutes. He was just in absolute joy. In fact, it was exactly as the Bible talks about. It was unspeakable joy and full of glory (see 1 Pet. 1:8)! When he got up, he was staggering around the room, barely able to stand because he was so drunk, just like the Bible describes how the disciples were affected at Pentecost (see Acts 2:1-21). He continued to stagger around, lifting his hands in the air and praising God repeatedly. This was a guy who was very analytical and had actually tried to get out of coming with me to the meeting. In fact, he was about as analytical as one could possibly imagine. I almost had to drag him there!

But when my buddy heard the word of God that night, it pierced his soul. The Bible says, *"For the word of God is living and powerful, and sharper than any two-edged sword, piercing even to the division of soul and spirit, and of joints and marrow, and is a discerner of the thoughts and intents of the heart"* (Heb. 4:12). The word of God prevails over intellect, and it cuts deep into one's soul and helps awaken the spirit. We had all gotten struck with a two-edged sword called the Book of Acts, and it cut all of us to the core! All I knew was that whatever he had, I wanted some of the same!

You see, folks, one thing I learned very quickly as a believer was that anything you ask for (according to God's will), in the name of Jesus, cannot be corrupted. Satan cannot interfere with the pipeline of the name of Jesus. My friend was experiencing a gift from God; a supernatural power from the heavens had come upon him. Immediately following, one of our other friends got up to be prayed for, and the exact same experience occurred with him!

A few days later, I went back over to this man's house for a meeting and had him pray for me. When he prayed for me, my life would never be the same. Our newfound friend asked the Holy Spirit of God to come upon me and endue me with power from on high. No sooner did he ask this of God then I felt the rush of lightning coming through the palms of my hands. I felt as if I had holes in my hands, and this rush of high-voltage electricity was surging through my body and traveling from my hands to my every member. I remember being so overcome by this power that I went to the ground. All I could do was bask in the glory of God because the Father was touching me in a way that I had never been previously touched. He was raining down on my life with power and fire that can only come from heaven. I began to laugh uncontrollably—a roaring laughter like a lion. I've never seen or heard a lion laugh; however, there is no other way to describe it. I tried to lift my head off the ground and a supernatural force pinned my head back to the ground, not allowing me to get up. Whether it was the Holy Spirit or an angel, I do not know; but it was one or the other who had pinned me to the floor. I tried to get up a second time, and this divine supernatural force would not let me get up. Now that I look back, I don't know why I would have ever wanted to get up, but I guess my carnal side was trying to get up and get on with the evening, but God was not through with me. Other than that, it is hard to explain the joy and reality of what happened that night. But one thing I do know: that Danny McDaniel had a different attitude about God when he got up off that ground.

It was at this point that I had the attitude that Peter and the rest of the disciples had after Pentecost. I no longer feared what man thought. I had a new boldness! I had what I call a "cut-my-head-off" mentality. You could cut my head off before I denied what Jesus had done in my life (see Acts 4).

Chapter 3

WHAT ABOUT PETER?

PETER'S HUMANITY AND BOLDNESS

Let's take a look at Peter's life and how he walked with Jesus, so that what I talked about in the last chapter makes a bit more sense. Jesus had three key disciples as part of His inner circle: Peter, James, and John. In fact, it was Peter who boldly confessed to Jesus that He was the Christ. And Jesus told Peter that He would build His church upon this rock, upon Peter and his confession of the Messiah (see Matt. 16:18).

You see, when you walk with Jesus and know that you are side by side with God in a flesh suit, you are going to be bold. Peter was allowed to go up to the Mount of Transfiguration and see Jesus talking with Moses and Elijah! Just imagine that. How would your faith be if you had been traveling with the Son of God for three years, twenty-four hours a day, seven days a week, with no television, no sporting events, no mass transportation, no elaborate hobbies available, and no electricity—nothing but Jesus? Imagine walking and spending three entire years with the Son of God and seeing the thousands of miracles that took place during this time. It was Peter who even briefly walked on water, something that only Jesus and Peter have done, according to all of my records (see Matt. 14:29).

Yes, Peter was bold as long as he was next to Jesus. Remember that it was Peter who said that he would die for Jesus, and Jesus had to remind him that he would deny Him three times before the cock crowed twice (see Mark 14:30). It was Peter who pulled the sword and cut off the ear of the servant of the high priest, while standing next to Jesus, in order to defend Him (see Mark 14:47). Keep in mind that all of this happened as he was physically next to Jesus.

But at the arrest of Jesus in the Garden of Gethsemane, the disciples scattered, including Peter. He followed the crowd into Jerusalem to find out what was going to become of his Master. It was then that Peter was faced with the brutal reality that he was only human. As long as Peter was physically with Jesus, he was bold and brave. However, things seemed to change when Jesus was arrested. He went on to deny Jesus three times, including cursing and claiming that he never knew Him. What would cause this fear to come upon him? What would cause a man who walked with the Son of God for three solid years, to totally deny his relationship with Him? What would cause a man sold out for Jesus to go back to his first love—fishing?

I believe that this account of Peter's life and his subsequent denial is a clear message from God: we can do nothing without Him. He tells us this in the Gospel of John (see John 15:5), and clarifies it in Matthew through the Book of Acts, that there is a second experience that must take place in order to walk in our true destiny while here on earth. What follows in the next chapter is a list of scriptures from Matthew through the Book of Acts that will help every born-again Christian understand that God was not finished with you when you believed in your heart and confessed with your mouth that Jesus is Lord. He is still working and desiring to empower you with His Holy Spirit, giving you boldness, just like Peter.

The question you must ask yourself is, "Do I want to be like the Peter who walked with Jesus, or do I want to be like the Peter who was transformed on the day of Pentecost?" Yes, it was the same man, but a man with a much deeper perspective of whom he walked with for three years. How long have you been walking with Christ? Would you like a much deeper perspective of who He is and what He intends to do with your life here on earth? This has nothing to with your eternal salvation, but it has everything to do with the way you are going to live out your destiny that God has planned for you while on earth. If Peter was with us today, I believe he would confess that he had some issues with pride, and I believe he would encourage us to humble ourselves and seek a deeper perspective of who God is and what His plans for us are.

SHOWING US THINGS WE DON'T KNOW

It is at this point that you must have the attitude that Diane and I had back in 1998 while attending the Lutheran church in the Austin area. "Lord, wherever You want us to be, take us there. Lord, whatever You have for us, we want it. We know there is more, so show us." We asked all of these things in Jesus's name, a name in which every knee must bow, in heaven, on the earth, and in the earth below (see Phil. 2:9-11). The Bible says in Jeremiah 33:3, *"Call to Me, and I will answer you, and show you great and mighty things, which you do not know."* Are you willing to call upon Him so that He can show you what He wants you to know?

Or will you close up this book right here, and cast all of this off as another one of those futile attempts of a heretic trying to deceive you? Before you make that choice, I encourage you to think about some of these things. Why are there more manifestations of supernatural things out there today involving the satanic kingdom than there are in the kingdom of God? Why do we see more power demonstrated by the powers of darkness than we do by the power of God? Is God incapable? You and I both know the answer to that. It is usually because of our unbelief that causes us to write off the possibility of experiencing more of God's power, giving credit to being deceived by something that appears to be an angel of light. Sometimes it has been ingrained in our head for so long to beware of false prophets, beware of satan appearing as angel of light, beware of false miracles, and beware of false tongues, that we are too quick to base all of our beliefs on what Brother Billy, or Aunt Suzie, or Grandma told us was the absolute truth, rather than find out for ourselves what the word of God says about these things.

In addition, there are Christian authors who are leading people astray by teaching them what is "not" available for Christians today. There are seminaries and professors that teach false doctrines and doctrines of demons because they believe that our God today does not operate the same way He did 2,000 years ago. And good, well-meaning believers fall for these teachings, hook, line, and sinker. They fall for these because these people have the "all important" seminary degree.

This reminds me of the exact biblical pattern of Jesus dealing with the Pharisees and Sadducees. Religious scholars during that time period mocked every move of the Holy Spirit because it did not match up to their religious training. Because they felt like they were experts and knew all they needed to know about God's word, they could quickly point out how wrong you were to believe that Jesus worked miracles. They could quickly shut down the fact that people who got healed must have been healed by some demonic means. And they could easily tell you that every supernatural experience you had must have been from the devil, because nothing in their religious upbringing allowed them to believe that Jesus is the same yesterday, today, and forever (see Heb. 13:8).

Am I indicating that we are to dishonor our parents, our pastors, our elders, and those that have gone before us? Absolutely not! I am just advocating that we trust in God with all of our heart, leaning not on our own understanding. There is a point in time when only God can reveal truth to you, and only God can launch you into your destiny. Jesus said, *"However, when He, the Spirit of truth, has come, He will guide you into all truth"* (John 16:13). My father and I always had a tremendous relationship, but if I would have restricted what I believed to be true solely on what my father taught me, I would have never stepped into my true destiny God had for me. God used all of the other people mentioned before, accompanied by my father, to help guide me into more of what was available to me through Christ Jesus.

I am appealing to you, right now, as you are reading this book, to lay all of your preconceived notions aside. I appeal to you to pray to the Lord Jesus to open your eyes and your heart to only what He has for you. I appeal to you to trust God and lay aside what you may have been taught by man that could be restricting you from all of the fullness God has for your life, and for the lives of all the people you know. I encourage you to pray this prayer before reading the detailed scriptures in the next chapter, which will lay out God's plan to bring a power into your life as a Christian that only He can bring to you:

Heavenly Father, in the name of Jesus, I come to You and ask You to open my eyes to Your truth, and Your truth only. I ask that You guard me from evil and deception, and I ask that You equip me with everything I need in order to live a victorious Christian life. If there is more that You have for me, I want to receive it. If there is more for me, then please reveal it to me. Father, I do not want anything to hold me back from fellowship with You. You said, "Call unto Me, and I will show you great and mighty things in which you do not know." Lord, I don't know everything; therefore, I am calling on You right now, in the name of Jesus, to show me great and mighty things in which I do not know. Amen.

Chapter 4

FINDING THE POWER

JESUS AND THE HOLY SPIRIT

This chapter has been designed to give you the scriptural foundations for understanding the promise of the Holy Spirit. It is important to understand that God is too good to send His only begotten Son to us as a sacrifice for our sins, to then leave us hanging by a thread as we live out the rest of our Christian lives. He promised us a Comforter, one who would help us in every area of our life. John the Baptist declared about the coming of Jesus:

> *I indeed baptize you with the water unto repentance, but He who is coming after me is mightier than I, whose sandals I am not worthy to carry. He will baptize you with the Holy Spirit and fire* (Matthew 3:11).

John the Baptist was the forerunner, the prophet, sent by God to bring repentance to His people. Along with that came a message of who was to come after him. It would be someone much greater. He would bring a baptism of the Holy Spirit and fire! This declaration will all tie in with the rest of scripture as we continue. But this first scripture is like a seed that needs to be planted in order for the word of God to cultivate in your heart.

There is a three-step process unfolding in this scripture:

- Repent—turn completely in the other direction from your sinful ways.

- Look to Jesus—He who is coming is mightier; John was merely the forerunner.

- Baptism of the Holy Spirit—He will baptize you with the Holy Spirit and with fire.

Remember that faith comes by hearing, and hearing by the word of God (see Rom. 10:17). It is only the word of God that will reveal truth to you, not a man such as me.

Before you read the next scripture that comes after the baptism of Jesus, I want you to ask yourself this question: "Did Jesus need to be baptized?" Absolutely not! He was God in the flesh. He did not have to be baptized like we are commanded to do. He was only baptized in order to fulfill all things. Jesus submitted Himself to baptism in order to model to us the next step after we believe, and that is to be baptized for the remission of sins. But something else happened as well:

And the Holy Spirit descended in bodily form like a dove upon Him, and a voice came from heaven which said, "You are My beloved Son; in You I am well pleased" (Luke 3:22).

Once again, you must ask this question: "Did Jesus need the Holy Spirit to descend upon Him like a dove?" Absolutely not! He was God in the flesh. But this happened to fulfill scripture—it was another model for the believer to take note of and learn from. The thing that we are to take note of is that the ministry of Jesus did not begin until the Holy Spirit descended upon Him like a dove. As we go through the scriptures in order, we will see that Jesus modeled everything perfectly for us, so that we would follow His model.

Luke writes, *"Then Jesus, being filled with the Holy Spirit, returned from the Jordan and was led by the Spirit into the wilderness..."* (Luke 4:1). It is important to take note that the Bible specifically states that Jesus, after being *filled* with the Holy Spirit, was now *led* by the Spirit. After the Holy Spirit had come upon Him after baptism, we see now the work of the Trinity in effect—Father, Son, and Holy Spirit working in unison.

JESUS'S TEACHING ON THE HOLY SPIRIT

So I say to you, ask, and it will be given to you; seek, and you will find; knock, and it will be opened to you. For everyone who asks receives, and he who seeks finds, and to him who knocks it will be opened.

If a son asks for bread from any father among you, will he give him a stone? Or if he asks for a fish, will he give him a serpent instead of a fish? Or if he asks for an egg, will he offer him a scorpion? If you being evil, know how to give good gifts to your children, **how much more will your heavenly Father give the Holy Spirit to those who ask Him!** (Luke 11:9-13)

In order for this scripture to sink into your heart, you must go back to the Bible and read the entire message Jesus was teaching, beginning in Luke 11. His disciples had asked Him how to pray. And Jesus finished with the above teaching.

But it began with what we call the Lord's Prayer, and this particular teaching that He gave His disciples ended with, *"how much more will your heavenly Father give the Holy Spirit to those who ask Him!"* Let's remember here that Jesus was talking to Christians. They were His disciples and they were asking Him how to pray. I believe this teaching was a foreshadowing of things to come. They might not have understood what He was really talking about until after He was gone, and they had to pray as He told them to later on.

Right before this, in Luke 11, Jesus had been teaching the disciples about being persistent about what they were asking for, even in the midnight hour—the whole illustration was based upon this fact. There are so many times that I have seen the Holy Spirit show up in our presence during the midnight hours and beyond while we were ministering. I believe that the Lord loves persistency, and He loves to see if His children will push through into the night, worshiping Him and seeking Him. It would do you well to read Luke 11 thoroughly and let it sink deep into your spirit. Read how Jesus really explains how to pray, and the kind of expectancy one should have when praying. And don't forget, He said, *"how much more will your heavenly Father give the Holy Spirit to those who ask Him!"* (Luke 11:13)

CLUES OF THE KINGDOM

On the last day, that great day of the feast, Jesus stood and cried out, saying, "If anyone thirsts, let him come to Me and drink. He who believes in Me, as the Scripture has said, out of his heart will flow rivers of living water." But this He spoke concerning the Spirit, whom those believing in Him would receive; for the Holy Spirit was not yet given, because Jesus was not yet glorified (John 7:37-39).

Once again, Jesus is giving clues to some of the mysteries of the kingdom of God. This scripture was a foreshadowing of things to come, of things that must happen after Jesus was glorified. But He said that rivers of living water would flow out of anyone's heart that is thirsty and believes in Him. He was referring to the Holy Spirit, which, in fact, is a promise to all who are thirsty and believe. Are you thirsty for Jesus? Do you believe in Him? If so, look and see, and examine what Jesus is promising to all who believe.

There is great revelation in this text. Jesus gave a three-part instruction for the Holy Spirit to come into a believer's life:

- If anyone thirsts

- Let him come to Me

- And drink

If you are thirsty, you are to come to Jesus and drink. I've never seen anyone drink with a closed mouth before. If you open your mouth and tell Jesus that you are thirsty, and you mean it, He will pour His Spirit upon you. I learned from the late Derek Prince, who was considered to be one of the most prominent biblical scholars of the twentieth century, that there is a real significance to looking up to heaven and opening your mouth. I have seen people pray for the Holy Spirit to come upon them with power from on high, and nothing of significance happened. Looking back, I realize that their mouths were closed! Since I received this revelation from the word of God, I have been amazed at how God responds to an open vessel (i.e., an open mouth).

JESUS'S PROMISED SPIRIT

Sometimes the scriptures are so simple and elementary that we miss it! That is probably why Jesus said that we must have the faith of a child to inherit the kingdom of God (see Mark 10:15). It is also probably why the Bible says that He would use the foolish things of this world to confuse the wise (see 1 Cor. 1:26-31). Just imagine what God really has in store for you. It is so magnificent and so glorious that the devil and his demon forces have been devising every scheme they can to keep you from your destiny. The devil has tried every deceptive tactic you could imagine to attempt to get Christians to outthink themselves. The devil is a liar, and now you have an incredible opportunity to begin approaching God with a childlike faith to receive all He has for you. One of those incredible gifts He has for you is His promise—the promise of the Holy Spirit! Jesus said:

> But the Helper, the Holy Spirit, whom the Father will send in My name, He will teach you all things, and bring to your remembrance all things that I said to you (John 14:26).

Here we have another foreshadowing of things to come. Jesus knew that there were certain things that He said which were prophetic in nature and would not be understood without the Holy Spirit coming into one's life. I have asked groups of people many times, "Have you ever daydreamed through reading two or three pages of the Bible and not even remember what you were reading?" Eyeballs seem to grow as people look at each other, knowing that it happens to them all the time. I also ask groups of people if they have a hard time understanding the scriptures, and get an overwhelming affirmative response. The point that I am trying to bring out to you is that when the Holy Spirit comes upon you, as the Bible teaches, your days of daydreaming through the Bible are over and your ability to comprehend scripture catapults you into another realm due to the Helper.

Jesus again promised:

Nevertheless I tell you the truth. It is to your advantage that I go away; for if I do not go away, the Helper will not come to you; but if I depart, I will send Him to you. And when He has come, He will convict the world of sin, and of righteousness, and of judgment: of sin, because they do not believe in Me; of righteousness, because I go to My Father and you see Me no more; of judgment, because the ruler of this world is judged.

I still have many things to say to you, but you cannot bear them now. However, when He, the Spirit of truth, has come, He will guide you into all truth; for He will not speak on His own authority, but whatever He hears He will speak; and He will tell you things to come (John 16:7-13).

It becomes quite clear when we read these scriptures and take God's word at face value, that God wants us to understand that the Holy Spirit will become an integral part of a believer's daily life. God's word points us toward an experience involving His power from heaven coming upon our life in order to equip us, sanctify us, and prepare for us for every good work.

Chapter 5

THE BELIEVER'S MANDATE

JESUS'S FIRST MANDATE

Jesus gave us plenty of evidence of the foreshadowing of things to come. He gave us the Gospels to bring us closer to Him and to give us an opportunity to believe in Christ Jesus. They were written to expose us to salvation, healing, and deliverance. The Greek word for salvation, healing, and deliverance is the same—sozo. It is an interchangeable word that describes what is to happen to the life of a believer in Jesus Christ when he or she is born again. That person, upon belief in Jesus, should be saved, healed, and delivered.

In fact, Jesus's first mandate for ministry as He sent out the original 12 disciples was, *"And as you go, preach, saying 'The kingdom of heaven is at hand.' Heal the sick, cleanse the lepers, raise the dead, cast out demons. Freely you have received, freely give"* (Matt. 10:7-8). Jesus had spent valuable time pouring

His wisdom and revelation knowledge into His disciples, and at this point He said, "Freely you have received, freely give."

JESUS' MODERN-DAY WORDS

Let me give you a modern-day illustration of what Jesus really meant when He issued the Great Commission. Jesus might have said, "Hey guys, everything that I have poured into your life, I did for a reason. Now I want you to go out and pour into the world everything I have put into you. I want you to be duplicatable. That's the point of discipleship. Whatever I do with you, I want you to do with others so that we can change the world. And, as you freely give to others, they will freely receive, and you will make disciples of them. It's all about duplication. If I have preached the gospel to you, then you are to preach this gospel to others. If I have taught you to heal the sick, then teach others to heal the sick by modeling it to them. If I have cast out devils, then you will cast out devils and model this ministry to them. If I have cleansed lepers and raised the dead, then you will stir up your faith to do the same things, modeling this to them. This process must be modeled, taught, and passed on because I have chosen not to do it all Myself.

"I will go to be with the Father one day, but I will send the Helper, the Holy Spirit, and He will guide you in all things. My purpose here is to model the process that the Father has set forth in order for you to turn people's hearts toward Me and toward Him. One day you will have to use My name because I will not be here; I am going to be with the Father, but you will do all of these things, even greater things, using My name. My name will give you the keys to the kingdom of heaven. Whatever you bind, or tie up, with your mouth on earth will be bound up in heaven. Whatever you loose, or command to be loosed, on earth will also be loosed in the heavenly realms. But you will use My name in order to do this. My name is the key, because no one gets to the Father except through Me. I hold the key.

"All power and authority has been granted to Me; however, I am giving you permission, and giving you a mandate, to use My name to do these things that I have modeled for you. You will literally have the power and authority to destroy the works of the devil, using My name, if you have eyes to see and ears to hear what I am teaching you. My Father sent Me here to destroy the works of the devil and you will continue to conquer and overcome his works using My name when I go the Father. The Helper, the Holy Spirit, will be with you, encouraging you to use the power of My name to do these things.

"This is the mandate—it is simple, so keep it simple—preach the gospel, heal the sick, cleanse the leper, raise the dead, and cast out demons. If people receive you, then they have received Me and believed in Me. If they do not receive you, then it will be more tolerable for the land of Sodom and Gomorrah in the day of judgment than for those who reject your ministry. You must be consistent, trust in Me, and not lean on your own understanding. I am teaching you rightly, as the Father has instructed Me."

GREAT COMMISSION = DUPLICATION

This example is obviously not scripture. However, it is proper emphasis added to what Jesus was doing in the lives of His disciples. He was creating a duplicatable, transferrable process in order to change humankind one person at a time. There is power in one: it even started with the power of one—Jesus. I have often said that Jesus is the author of network marketing! Jesus discipled a few men to learn how to build nets in order to network, so that His net works! The Great Commission is all about duplication. If disciples duplicate what was taught to them by the visionary, and fight to preserve the vision of the visionary, then the vision will remain clear. If disciples, somewhere along the way, begin to alter the vision or take shortcuts, then the vision becomes distorted. I believe Jesus made it very clear to all of humankind how He wanted His ministry to be modeled in order to build the church.

In His last words, before He ascended to the Father, He told them:

And He said to them, "Go into all the world and preach the gospel to every creature. He who believes and is baptized will be saved; but he who does not believe will be condemned. And these signs will follow those who believe: In My name they will cast out demons; they will speak with new tongues; they will take up serpents; and if they drink anything deadly, it will by no means hurt them; they will lay hands on the sick, and they will recover."

So then, after the Lord had spoken to them, He was received up into heaven, and sat down at the right hand of God. And they went out and preached everywhere, the Lord working with them and confirming the word through the accompanying signs. Amen (Mark 16:15-20).

I want you to see through scripture that it is very important to recognize the initial mandate Jesus gave His leaders. These were the first words for the ministry model, and they also were His last words for the model of ministry in which they were to follow. I want you to imagine that if you knew you were going to go to heaven tomorrow, and you have a spouse and children, what would you say to them in your last words? What kind of instruction would you give them? What legacy would you leave them with?

Knowing that He was going to ascend to His throne in heaven, Jesus took this opportunity to remind His disciples exactly what He had commissioned them to do in His original mandate. I want you to know that this was a mandate, not a recommendation. The word mandate means "a formal order from a superior court or official to an inferior one."[1] Jesus is the King of kings, and He issued a royal command to His disciples before leaving this earth.

The ministry model of Jesus is clearly laid out in these two passages, which happen to be the "first" words of Jesus in regards to releasing the disciples into the ministry field, and the "last" words of Jesus, reminding His disciples of the Great Commission. The Bible has been given to us not merely as a history book, but as the bread of life in which we are to eat from and feed others who do not know about this Man, Jesus. These words are living words, applicable to today, because Jesus is the same yesterday, today, and forever, just as the Bible states (see Heb. 13:8).

Jesus said, *"And these signs will follow those who believe"* (Mark 16:17). I often ask other Christians, "Do you believe?" If you believe, then why aren't these signs following you? It does not say, "These signs might follow those who believe." These signs should surround the life of a true believer. This is really a very clear mandate given by Jesus. If one does not believe this to be true, then they need to throw their Bible in the trashcan! For John says in God's word:

> *For I testify to everyone who hears the words of the prophecy of this book: If anyone adds to these things, God will add to him the plagues that are written in this book; and if anyone takes away from the words of the book of this prophecy, God shall take away his part from the Book of Life, from the holy city, and*

from the things which are written in this book (Revelation 22:18-19).

Wow! Is that not enough to want to obey the Lord?

NOTE

1. "Mandate." Webster's Third New International Dictionary, Unabridged. Merriam-Webster, 2002. http://unabridged.merriam-webster.com (11 Mar. 2012).

Figure 2

MARK 16:15-18

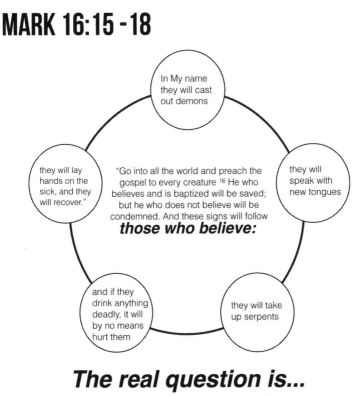

In My name they will cast out demons

they will lay hands on the sick, and they will recover."

"Go into all the world and preach the gospel to every creature ¹⁶ He who believes and is baptized will be saved; but he who does not believe will be condemned. And these signs will follow *those who believe:*

they will speak with new tongues

and if they drink anything deadly, it will by no means hurt them

they will take up serpents

The real question is... do you believe?

¹⁵ And He said to them, "Go into all the world and preach the gospel to every creature. ¹⁶ He who believes and is baptized will be saved; but he who does not believe will be condemned. ¹⁷ And these signs will follow those who believe: In My name they will cast out demons; they will speak with new tongues; ¹⁸ they will take up serpents; and if they drink anything deadly, it will by no means hurt them; they will lay hands on the sick, and they will recover."
Luke 16:15

Figure 1

Chapter 6

THE SIGNS THAT FOLLOW BELIEVERS

THE NAME OF JESUS PREVAILS

The first sign Jesus mentions in Mark 16 is the visible sign of casting out demons by a believer. I have seen thousands upon thousands of demons flee from people's lives. I say this humbly because I know that I can do nothing without Him. However, the same Spirit that raised Jesus from the dead dwells in me; therefore, I know that I am able to perform all the works Jesus mandated me to perform by faith.

I have had demons speak to me through the mouth of the person in whom I was ministering, threatening to kill me or kill my family. However, I know that the devil is a liar and that the Bible says, *"No weapon formed against you shall prosper, and every tongue which rises up against you in judgment you shall condemn"* (Isa. 54:17). I have had demons laugh at me and mock me, but the name of Jesus has always prevailed. They can mock me, but they can't mock Jesus!

There is a story from the Book of Acts about some Jews who were not followers of Christ and who had seen enough of the ministry of Paul that they had become curious enough to attempt to cast demons out of people. The only problem was that they were not Christians! They were only curious. Here is how the story reads from Acts 19:13-20:

> Then some of the itinerant Jewish exorcists took it upon themselves to call the name of the Lord Jesus over those who had evil spirits, saying, "We exorcise you by the Jesus whom Paul preaches." Also there were seven sons of Sceva, a Jewish chief priest, who did so.
>
> And the evil spirit answered and said, "Jesus I know, and Paul I know; but who are you?"
>
> Then the man in whom the evil spirit was leaped on them, overpowered them, and prevailed against them, so that they fled out of that house naked and wounded. This became known both to all Jews and Greeks dwelling in Ephesus; and fear fell on them all, and the name of the Lord Jesus was magnified. And many who had believed came confessing and telling their deeds. Also, many of those who had practiced magic brought their books together and burned them in the sight of all.

And they counted up the value of them, and it totaled fifty thousand pieces of silver. So the word of the Lord grew mightily and prevailed.

This situation proved that only a believer, or follower of Jesus Christ, has the ability to cast a demon out of someone; and it also proves how the reality of the supernatural can affect multitudes of people. Because devout Jews saw that their priests had no power to exorcise demons out of another person, yet ordinary and "untrained" men could cast demons out of a person in the name of Jesus, several things happened:

- Fear of the Lord fell upon many of the people.

- The name of the Lord Jesus was magnified.

- Witchcraft books were destroyed at the rate of 50,000 pieces of silver!

- And the word of the Lord grew mightily and prevailed.

MIRACLE-DRIVEN CHURCH

This is an example of how badly we need the power of the Holy Spirit in our lives. If you want to know the fastest way to grow a church, this is it. The problem with many pastors who have been called by God to build His church today is that they want to learn how to grow a church from all the seminars and conferences in which they attend. They will jump from one conference to the next, strategizing on how to bring large numbers of people into their church on Sunday. Sometimes, it is so they can be seen as one of the fastest growing churches in America or even the world. It falls under the guise of being concerned about souls, but deep down there is a desire for some pastors to be significant "players" in the ministry world. In most of these cases, it takes a lot of things centered around programs and extraordinary audio/video presentations in order to attract the people on a week-by-week basis. They then justify it by the times that we live in. Most pastors in America would never buy into the fact that a miracle-driven church, powered and governed by the Holy Spirit, could multiply and hold large numbers on a weekly basis.

The litmus test for this is, Does this church cast out demons? If the answer is no, then there is a theological issue here and it doesn't align with God's word. This passage from Acts 19 gives us a biblical justification of the fact that God's plan for multiplication is the same today as it was 2,000 years ago. I have seen it firsthand. When unsaved people get into an atmosphere in which the "signs that follow those who believe" are in effect, they are in awe of the power of God. I have witnessed this firsthand since 2001, when God changed my life forever.

FOREVER CHANGED

I'll never forget a two-night conference I preached at in Abilene, Texas, in the spring of 2005. There were

14 male college students whom I had taken through a weekend retreat a couple of months prior, and all 14 of them were from Baptist and Church of Christ denominations. They all loved the Lord and they all wanted to grow in Christ. During our weekend together, 12 out of the 14 young men had demons cast out of them, and most of them received the promise of the Holy Spirit following their experience. They were so excited that they wanted me to come to Abilene and tell all their friends about the real ministry of Jesus—the Great Commission.

The first night of ministry in Abilene, they put 85 people in the room, all from Baptist and Church of Christ backgrounds. The next night there were 110 people in the room for the final teachings. At the end of the second night, I issued an altar call, asking for anybody to come up who wanted to be free from any demonic oppression in their lives. It was silent! For a couple of minutes, nobody moved. I could tell that scores of people wanted to run up to the front, but it seemed as if no one wanted to be the guinea pig! Finally, one young man came up and told me that he wanted to be set free. I do not remember what it was in particular that he wanted freedom from, but I do remember casting demons out of him. Afterward, I explained to all 110 people what had taken place, and how simple God's plan for freedom was—then the rush was on. I had a line of people waiting for prayer to be set free from various demonic oppressions. No one was leaving or trying to make a run for the nearest door!

At the end of the night, around 2:00 a.m., there was a young college student who waited until everyone was out of the facility before he had me sit down with him and told me his story. He told me how he had sat there for two nights and listened to me preach, and how he watched all of those people obtain new measures of freedom in Christ. And he told me how he was a homosexual, and that he now understood that God did not make him a homosexual. He said he totally understood that the enemy had somehow been able to come into his life by means of a homosexual spirit (which is a sexually perverted spirit). He said he loved Jesus but wanted to be set free from homosexuality. There was a lot more to the conversation than that. But the point of the story was that he saw miracles! Because this young man saw the Holy Spirit of God working through demonstrations of power, he knew he had the hope to overcome a lifestyle in which the Lord convicted him of as being wrong. He didn't have me condemning him. He didn't hear me preaching about homosexuals being lesser human beings, or being evil for that matter. He didn't hear me say or do anything that made him feel like he wasn't loved just as much as I was loved. But he did hear me preach the gospel, and he saw the signs that followed those who believe. The next step was to cast the sexually perverted spirit out of him, allowing him to walk out of that facility that night knowing that Jesus is real and God is a God of power.

UNDERSTANDING UNCLEAN SPIRITS

Once a believer begins to understand what an unclean spirit is, and what its particular assignment is, then we begin to better understand why Jesus tells us to cast them out. For example, an alcoholic *has* to have another drink because the spirit of alcoholism, or the spirit of addiction, is speaking to him from inside his body, in the realm of the soul. The spirit is operating in his mind, will, and emotions, and this is what prompts him to "have another drink." It is not a spirit out on a limb of a tree, yelling at him, "Hey, you need to pick up a bottle of vodka on the way home!" It is not a spirit sitting on the couch next to him watching football that says, "Hey, you need to go get another beer out of the refrigerator!" The spirit is speaking to him from within; therefore, it must be cast out. This is why your local liquor store sign usually reads, "Wine & Spirits." You pay for the liquor, but you get the spirits for free! Well, at least on the front end.

I know exactly what the "spiritual" Christian is thinking right now! Many people who consider themselves to be "spiritual" are thinking, "All you ever see is a bunch of weird people talking about stuff like this, or doing stuff like this." For the most part, you are right! Don't think for one second that the devil has not done his very best to discount the supernatural acts of God over the past 2,000 years. I can tell you with all sincerity that the Holy Spirit is not weird! God is not weird! And Jesus is not weird! As long as you don't act weird, you will draw in the multitudes. On that particular night in Abilene, Texas, I do not remember one single person walking out of the room when they saw the first miracle. The reason for that was that I represented the Holy Spirit with humility and honor without being flaky.

WEIRDNESS AND CHURCH LEADERSHIP

In fact, I will write about weirdness for a moment. There comes a point and time in our life when we have to give up on the fact that everyone is not going to be exactly like us. Everyone is not going to dress as good as you do. Everyone is not going to style his or her hair as nice as you do. Everyone is not going to look as appealing as you do. If we look at the life of John the Baptist, we see a man preaching that the kingdom of heaven was drawing near, dressed in camel's hair with a leather belt around his waist. He came to us eating locusts and wild honey; so we all have to understand that God will get His message through to the people because it is His message. Our job is not to miss the message because of the messenger.

I admit to you that I struggle with some of these same issues myself. There are many times that I have been in a church and seen people acting strange or weird, but what I have to continually remind myself is, "My job is to focus on God, not other people." We sure don't think it's weird when we see a bunch of guys painting their faces to attend a football game. We don't think it's weird when we see people running across the football stadium waving flags. We sure don't think it's weird to see everybody raise their hands to the school song when giving honor to their school. And we sure don't think it's weird to see people jumping up and down, screaming and shouting at sporting events as they root for their favorite teams. But, we have a much different perspective of how we believe church behavior should be as we come to honor and praise the King of all kings. This doesn't mean that we should have churches out of order, or people should have a license to act weird and wacky during church. It is the role of the pastor, the elders, and the deacons to handle all of the church government, under the clear direction of the Holy Spirit.

I have currently seen a trend in the way that men in the church are dressing and do not agree with it. I believe with all of my heart that the enemy has launched a direct attack on the church by influencing church leaders, such as pastors and worship leaders, to dress more feminine than ever. When my wife and I flew through London on the way to Africa in 2005, I sensed that this attack was coming to America. I told my wife that there was about to be a launch of European feminization upon America in regards to men's clothing—Europe was trying to feminize men in America with their clothing, and it was going to affect the church. I believed it was going to cause people to turn from the church because of the male leaders in the church looking so feminine in all of their clothing styles.

It is now 2012, and I see so many of our church leaders falling into this very trap. Because other leaders wear these ultra-feminine clothes, American church leaders tend to dress just like them. Here is where duplication kicks in. You have young males in junior high and high school dressing ultra-feminine because their role models dress ultra-feminine. Many church leaders will justify this by explaining that all of the lost and hurting kids out there dress like this, so it makes them easier to reach because everybody looks alike. First of all, all of the lost and hurting kids don't dress feminine. Secondly, our job is to see them transformed, not transform ourselves just so one particular group of kids will show up for pizza every week while we hope our watered-down gospel message eventually sinks in with them. Those same kids are not looking for a feminine male church leader to model femininity to them so that they can have permission to preach the gospel to them. Those kids are looking for something supernatural to fill the void in their life, which is usually a gaping hole in their heart from abuse or neglect. Those same kids, as I write this book, are spending over $40 million per week in America to see the next vampire movie. They are looking for an experience, and our God has much more supernatural power than any form of witchcraft like *Harry Potter* or a *Twilight* movie. The problem is that they have never seen or heard of any other such power. We, as the church, ought to be ashamed at the job we have done of showing people the real Jesus and the authentic Great Commission.

These young men are looking for a male role model who can teach them how to be a warrior, a conqueror. If you track all of the media that goes into their eye gates, you will find that most of it has to do with combat, conquering, and warring in some fashion. The next generation is desperately seeking male leadership and male role models. If you are a male leader, it is your responsibility to make sure you look like a real man, accompanied by strength, humility, and love. I am not going to define what a "real man" ought to look like. It carries a loose interpretation, and one should not be legalistic; however, the easiest gauge is to not look "feminine"!

GOD CAN USE ANYONE

Even with all that I have just said, I have to realize that I am not God. If God can use a man dressed in camel's hair to pave the way for Jesus Christ to begin His ministry and even baptize Jesus, then God can use a man dressed in ultra-feminine clothing. It almost sounds contradictory when you think about what I said in the preceding paragraphs, but there is a valid point to this emphasis. We have to be very careful not to judge or condemn fellow believers without due cause. What is important for all of us to remember is what Paul the apostle taught us about doing our best to be appealing to all types of people for the purpose of not being a stumbling block in someone's life. He stated that *"to the weak I became as weak, that I might win the weak. I have become all things to all men, that I might by all means save some"* (1 Cor. 9:22). In Paul's letter to the Corinthians, he describes in greater detail how he became weak to reach the weak, and how he became as a Jew in order to reach the Jews. The real key here is balance.

However, I believe that all church leaders must understand that the world is watching them all of the time, and that as they go, so goes the church. Our job as Christian leaders is to raise up the next generation in the love and fear of the Lord. I believe that God is mobilizing His last-day army of warriors, equipping them to fight the good fight of faith like never before, and that will entail having a warrior spirit, not a feminine spirit. God is calling men to rise up to a higher level of manhood while maintaining the humility necessary to bring glory to the King. We have not been called to compromise and have people guessing as to what sexual preferences we have. We have been called to bring glory to God.

THE SPIRIT BRINGS POWER, LIGHT, AND FIRE

You might be asking yourself, "What does this have to do with the promise of the Holy Spirit?" The answer to that question is, "Everything!" The Holy Spirit brings power!

We live in a world today where demonstrations of the power of God are needed more than ever. The Bible says, *"For our gospel did not come to you in word only, but also in power, and in the Holy Spirit and in much assurance, as you know what kind of men we were among you for your sake"* (1 Thess. 1:5). It is the presence and power of the Holy Spirit that attracts people toward you. People are desperately seeking light. They really don't want to turn to the darkness, but they have to witness power in the light. In fact, it takes power to generate light. The lights in our home do not come on, nor are they sustained, without a power source. God has called us to be a light shining before all men, and we need a power source from which to both generate and sustain that light. That can only come from the Holy Spirit, and He wants you to have a significant portion of His power source.

Almost all of the living creatures I can think of are drawn to the light. Bugs are always attracted to the nearest light when it is dark out. Fish are always drawn toward lights in the water. Animals tend to be drawn toward light, because where there is light, there is heat. That's why John the Baptist said, *"He who is coming after me is mightier than I...He will baptize you with the Holy Spirit and fire"* (Matt. 3:11). The Holy Spirit brings light into your life, but He also brings fire! He brings the necessary heat to warm people up to God's word. He brings the heat that can cause the word of God to come off of your lips like a powerful, two-edged sword! He brings enough fire to burn up and extinguish all of the fiery darts of the enemy. He brings the kind of fire that will cause demons to flee from people's lives and find another place to dwell.

Hollywood has been somewhat accurate in some of the depictions of evil in this world. Demons hate the light because only truth can remain in the light. Vampires, in vampire movies, can only function in the dark because they cannot handle the light. Light brings the heat that burns up the enemy and destroys him. This is an elementary illustration of how we need the Holy Spirit functioning at a high level in our life. What Christian would not want to have an opportunity to be a vessel for the power and fire of the Holy Spirit?

Prior to knowing about and receiving the promise of the Holy Spirit, I had never considered casting a demon out of another human being. But immediately following my experience of receiving the promise of the Holy Spirit, I did not hesitate to help others in need and who had any sort of demonic oppression. Once the power of God came upon my life, I could not help but have a desire to fulfill God's purpose for my life. My life was brighter. I had more light, and there was more power flowing through the earthly vessel of my body. God's purpose for my life is to preach the gospel, heal the sick, cleanse the leper, raise the dead, and cast out demons. Freely I have received from Him, and freely I give back to others (see Matt. 10:7-8).

Chapter 7

MORE SIGNS THAT FOLLOW

ARGUMENTS AGAINST TONGUES?

Jesus said that speaking in tongues is another sign that should follow believers (see Mark 16:17), and the apostle Paul emphasized this in his teachings as well (see 1 Cor. 12–14). I have both spoken and continue to speak in other tongues and utter mysteries unto God, just like Paul taught to the Corinthian church (see 1 Cor. 14:1-5). Most religious people who depend more on the doctrines and traditions of men would say that tongues are of the devil. I served the devil faithfully for 13 years and I never spoke in another tongue during that time!

Some people are taught that the spiritual gifts of prophecy and tongues, which are manifestations of the Holy Spirit, disappeared after the death of the last apostle. One question I have always had is, "Who in the world was the last apostle?" Apostles have not ceased to exist. The Bible describes five different offices of ministry, which are the apostle, the prophet, the teacher, the evangelist, and the pastor (see Eph. 4:11). One can't say that pastors, evangelists, and teachers still exist but God did away with the apostles and prophets. But some people do say that, and I would advise you to run from those people who lead Christians astray.

Other arguments lean toward accusing people who speak in unknown tongues of speaking in false tongues. There is an elementary level answer for this: for every action there is an equal and opposite reaction. If there is a false, then there must be a true. You can't have a counterfeit dollar bill unless there are some real dollar bills to copy. You can't have false tongues unless there are real tongues that exist. Someone out there is speaking mysteries unto God, according to First Corinthians 14, and it could be you! However, if you do not believe that God can supernaturally give you another "tongue" to speak in, you don't have to worry because He won't bother you with it.

ALL YOU NEED IS LOVE

In regards to tongues ceasing with the death of the last apostle, most people misunderstand what Paul later taught in the first book of Corinthians about the passing of spiritual gifts. He did talk about this issue and stated that everything would pass away, except love. Here is what Paul said:

Love never fails. But whether there are prophecies, they will fail; whether there are tongues, they will cease; whether there is knowledge, it will vanish away. For we know in part and we prophesy in part. But when that which is perfect has come, then that which is in part will be done away (1 Corinthians 13:8-10).

The other theological flaw in this particular doctrinal belief is that these "experts" teach Christians that prophecy and tongues have been done away with; however, they do not teach that knowledge has ceased. Knowledge is contained in the same exact verse as the prophecy and tongues ceasing! In essence, it is really a false doctrine, and the demons love it when Christian teachers instruct others with these false interpretations of scripture.

It is peculiar that these stiff-necked biblical scholars that we put so much trust in teach people that tongues and prophecy have ceased, but they fail to teach that knowledge ceased as well. They use what I call the "pick-and-choose" method of believing God's word. That means that "I am going to pick and choose what I believe to be true in order to justify what I believe. Anything outside of my beliefs must be wrong because I have never experienced it. Since I love God so much, and I haven't experienced anything beyond what I currently believe, then it must be false. It has to be false because I love God so much and He loves me so much that He would have already given me everything I needed to live a sanctified, powerful, pure, and holy life."

The easy part here is understanding that tongues, prophecy, and knowledge will be done away with only when that which is perfect has come. Obviously, Paul was talking about Jesus since He is the only perfect there is. Since Jesus had already come prior to Paul's arrival on the scene, he is clearly referring to the second coming of Christ. Basically, what Paul is saying is that you can't take tongues to heaven with you because you don't need them in heaven. Heaven is perfect. You don't need prophecy in heaven because heaven is perfect. Nor do you need knowledge in heaven—heaven is perfect. All you will need is love! Love gets to go with you because love is perfect. And God is love. And the Bible also says that God is perfect: *"Therefore you shall be perfect, just as your Father in heaven is perfect"* (Matt. 5:48). But until you get to heaven, you will need to speak in tongues, you will need prophecy, and you will need knowledge.

UTILIZING THE GIFTS GOD'S GIVEN YOU

Therefore, until Jesus comes back, or until you die and go to heaven, you will have access to tongues, prophecy, and knowledge. It will be up to you to utilize what you have access to. We have a lot of things in life in which we have access to, but we make choices as to whether or not we want to use those things. The same will hold true for you with spiritual gifts. Jesus has given you the keys to the kingdom. You have access to tongues in order to speak mysteries unto God; however, you have to take the key (the name of Jesus) and open the door to the supernatural.

Paul said, *"For he who speaks in a tongue does not speak to men but to God, for no one understands him; however, in the spirit he speaks mysteries"* (1 Cor. 14:2). This is good news! Will it not be a wonderful thing when God comes upon you with power from heaven and releases the manifestation of the gift of tongues in your life? You will have the ability to speak directly to your Father in heaven! You will be uttering mysteries, yet God will know exactly what you are praying for.

For me personally, experience has shown that when I pray in another tongue to God, I do not pray selfishly because I do not know what I am praying. I also do not have to think about what I need to pray for or want to pray about because the Spirit speaks through me.

In 2002 we moved to Brentwood, Tennessee, and our house backed up to a shallow river called the Little Harpeth. The Little Harpeth, under normal conditions, was like a creek with pools and shallow water running throughout the riverbed. In most places, one can walk in knee-deep water and then come upon a pool of three to five feet of water to swim in. We have three boys, and at the time they were 11, 7, and 3. Our boys are all outdoorsmen and sports fanatics, so you can imagine how much they liked the river in the backyard as kids.

Shortly after moving to Brentwood, our middle son, Gavin, came running up to the back of the house one afternoon screaming and crying that, our oldest, Cam was dead (our oldest)! I had been walking the river with the boys about 30 minutes before, now my middle son was hysterical, and I still have never seen fear and hysteria on a human being like I witnessed that day. My wife and I immediately dropped whatever we were doing and began to sprint to the river. As soon as I took off, I began to cry out in tongues. I was sprinting and screaming in tongues at the very same moment. I ran about 100 yards to the river and continued to run through the water for about a quarter to half a mile searching for my son's body. I never, for one second, quit screaming in tongues the entire time. Fortunately, we found Cam about a half-mile down the river talking to one of his new classmates and his classmate's father. Gavin was only 7, and he had just lost sight of Cam and did not know what to think. However, the important thing to understand is that I was crying out to God for my child whom I did not want to find floating in the river. When you need God desperately, your unknown tongue will be the tongue you rely on to communicate with the Father.

It is very hard for me to try and make this sound logical to someone who has never spoken in another tongue—it is like trying to explain what it is like to have a son or a daughter to someone who has never had a child. It is like trying to explain how beautiful Bora Bora is to someone who has never been there. It's just good news, and it is something that you want to experience in this life! It will enrich your life.

I have seen and heard tongues spoken in a heavenly language, and I have also seen and heard demonic tongues spoken. The devil aims to pervert every perfect gift that the Lord has created. Because of that, he brings false tongues into the world to infiltrate people's lives wherever he can gain access. The circulation of counterfeit money has not kept you from having the confidence to spend your real money. So why should people speaking in false tongues stop you from pursuing the real thing? Yes, there are counterfeit tongues used in the world today, but it should not stop you from desiring to speak in an unknown tongue given to you by the Holy Spirit. Whatever God gives you, via the Holy Spirit, is real and meant to be used.

Chapter 8

SERPENTS AND POISONS

"Taking up serpents" is not snake handling (see Mark 16:18)! Taking up serpents simply describes our power over the enemy and our ability to exercise control over demonic powers that try to thwart the plans of God in our lives. I have seen and used this authority that was granted to us by Jesus Christ many times. He gave us the keys to the kingdom. The name of Jesus is the key, which is the name above all names!

SNAKE BITES HEALED

I have witnessed one of my young nephews get instantly healed after being bit by a mature copperhead snake at my house in 2008. My 16-year-old son, Cam, and my sister, laid hands on him, prayed the exact scriptures listed above from Mark 16 over his life, and was healed. When we arrived at the hospital, his parents were in the emergency room with smiles on their faces. Their son had two bite marks on his leg, a little bit of bruising and redness, but no ill effects from the poison. He never received anti-venom or any other treatment because he was supernaturally healed by the power of Jesus Christ!

I am not attempting to give my son and my sister any special credit here, especially over his parents. But I do want you to see the point I'm trying to make. My son and my sister had the word of God inside of them. They knew the scriptures about the signs that are to follow believers. They acted upon these scriptures because they trusted the word of God. My son believes what God says, not what some preacher said because of what he learned not to believe in his seminary training. Because my son and my sister had the word of God in their hearts, it flowed out of them and became life for another human being. My nephew's parents were also praying the same way, but they were not on site. They were at another couple's house, having a prayer meeting. A unique twist to the story is that one of the friends at the prayer meeting had just stated, "I can't wait until we see the days where we begin to see the signs of the believer really take effect."[1]

As soon as the words came out of his mouth, my niece's cell phone rang and she got the news about her son's snakebite. Because God's word travels from the natural realm into the heavenly realm, their prayers were just as effective as the other prayers! My sister (the grandmother) who was on site drove the car to the hospital, and she was praying the same prayer based on the word of God in the 16th chapter of

Mark. Overall, you had a group of people, all believing God's word, not what someone taught them not to believe by some pastor who teaches that our God is not capable of doing the same thing for us as He did for Paul the apostle on the isle of Malta.

When Paul was shipwrecked on the island of Malta, the natives had shown them kindness by making a fire because it was a cold and rainy (see Acts 28:1-6). Paul had gathered some extra sticks to put on the fire, and when he laid the sticks on the fire, the heat caused a viper to come up out of the pile of wood and it bit him on the arm. Paul shook the snake off, and the natives knew that he was staring at death. They considered him to be a murderer that was being judged accordingly because of the poisonous bite. But when they watched Paul for a long time and realized that no swelling or harm had come to him, they believed he was a god. This is the power over the enemy that Jesus was talking about as He reminded His disciples and gave them the Great Commission (see Luke 10:17-20; Matt. 28:18-20). This is exactly why my young nephew did not swell up and was without harm. Case studies from the Bible showed that he would be just fine. When we study the ultimate medical book, we can make some unusual discoveries.

POISON SHALL NOT HARM YOU

I have seen one of my sons, as an infant, drinking from a bottle of bleach that was lying on the floor while the house was being cleaned. I also witnessed that poison having no ill effect on him. Jesus said, *"And if they drink anything deadly, it will by no means hurt them"* (Mark 16:18). We began praying Mark 16 over his life immediately, and he was fine.

Now God's word is not for us to play with. We should never tempt or try the Lord God on His word. He does not give us permission to play with poison or amuse ourselves with snakes. He simply gives us protection from the devil and his plans to steal, kill, and destroy our lives. In context, I believe this portion of scripture was worded in such a way because a common method of murder during those times was to put poison in one's drink. I believe Jesus was reassuring Christians that no deadly poison was going to be the cause of death for a Spirit-filled, gospel-preaching disciple of Christ.

There have been numerous times in the past few years, since we have received the promise of the Holy Spirit, in which we were exposed to sickness and disease. We see people walk around in fear of drinking from the same cup as a friend or relative, or fearful of diseases being spread various ways through the atmosphere. We hold on to the clear message of scripture that no deadly poison will hurt us. We have seen a lot of kids get strep throat in school, yet our kids remain healthy. We have seen parents worry about our kids being around their kids, or worry about our kids drinking from someone's cup because of strep throat, the flu, or some other sickness; however, we do not worry about these things attacking us due to our faith in God. Don't get me wrong, our kids have battled a slight illness a time or two in their lives—but they really have been slight. As long as we are preaching the gospel, and giving God 100 percent of the glory, we can be assured that there will be signs that follow us. Those signs will follow us because the Bible says that those signs follow those who believe.

I have seen hundreds of people healed from all kinds of sicknesses and diseases. I'll never forget the time when my wife and I first started living out these principles in 2001, because our 9-year-old son, Cam, had a serious bout with poison ivy. He woke up around midnight and could not sleep due to the severe irritation on his rear end. I came to his bedroom, checked on him, and found that his entire rear end had red welts all over it. The welts were creeping down the back and inside of his legs as well. It was an awful sight, and I have personally never seen a worse case of poison ivy—it was really ugly. Most parents would have taken their child to the hospital upon the sight of what I was looking at. He was in severe pain.

I asked him, "Do you know that God says that 'no deadly poison can harm you'?" And I went on to tell him that Jesus could heal him that night and make the poison ivy go away. He told me that he believed the same thing, and that he wanted Jesus to take the pain and itching away. So we prayed together, and I proclaimed healing over his body, specifically proclaiming Mark chapter 16 over his life. He immediately fell back asleep, which was supernatural in and of itself, and the next morning when he woke up, all of the welts were completely gone. There was no sign he had ever had poison ivy! Stories like this get me excited and make me want to go out and minister to people!

NOTE

1. This statement is slightly paraphrased due to memory and time lapse.

Chapter 9

HEALING POWER

Jesus also told His disciples that those who believe *"will lay hands on the sick, and they will recover"* (Mark 16:18). Christians who have a problem with this issue just don't understand the meaning of the scriptures. This scripture, in its original text, is stated like this: "You will lay hands on the sick and they will go through the process of recovery." Sometimes healing occurs instantly, due to the dunamis power of God—dunamis being the Greek word translated as "dynamite." There are many times when people are instantly healed, and there are other times when people go through the process of healing.

THE PROCESS OF HEALING

The very first person that my wife and I ever prayed for to receive divine healing occurred just days after we both received the promise of the Holy Spirit. One morning, as I was in my closet praying, and the Spirit of God spoke to me (not audibly, but to my spirit) and instructed me to get up and go to the phone and call one of our friends who had been diagnosed with a two-pound tumor in her stomach. The tumor was the size of a large grapefruit. Our friend lived over two hours away, but God had told me to call her and ask if Diane and I could come to see her so that we could pray with her and encourage her. She was very welcoming to our proposal, so we got in the car and took off. Just minutes from her and her husband's home, the Holy Spirit prompted me to pull over at a major grocery store, purchase a bottle of olive oil, and for my wife and I to pray for the oil to be anointed by God. I did not know a thing about anointing oil at this time, but the Holy Spirit knows everything! Jesus said, *"But the Helper, the Holy Spirit, whom the Father will send in My name, He will teach you all things"* (John 14:26).

We reached our friend's home and ministered the word of God to her and her husband for about two hours. They were both Christians, but neither one of them had ever heard that cancer and tumors were of demonic origins, nor had they heard of the power of the Holy Spirit. After teaching the word to them, she was desperate for a miracle of healing. We told her that we were going to cast out the unclean spirits associated with her tumor, such as infirmity and cancer, and then we were going to anoint her with oil and command healing to take place in her body. She agreed with us wholeheartedly, so my wife and I cast out several demons that were responsible for bringing that huge tumor to her, and then we prayed for her to be completely healed.

It wound up being a miraculous day, and our friend just knew that God was with all of us in those hours. We departed from them in peace and rejoiced in her healing. About six days later I received a phone call from her, and she was discouraged. She told me that she wanted to believe that God healed her, but she could still feel the grapefruit-sized tumor in her stomach, and she was still experiencing pain.

Praise God that I was a total novice when it came to the ministry of healing, because the Bible says, *"But when they arrest you and deliver you up, do not worry beforehand, or premeditate what you will speak. But whatever is given you in that hour, speak that; for it is not you who speak, but the Holy Spirit"* (Mark 13:11). I had no idea how to respond to our friend who had the symptoms of an existing tumor and who was highly discouraged. The good news is that the Holy Spirit spoke for me, and gave me the exact words of encouragement that she needed. I told her something to the effect, "Girl, you just have faith. Diane and I sowed seeds of healing into your body last week. Those were just seeds, but God will bring the harvest. So just remain strong in your faith and believe that He will finish the job."

The next day my wife and I were driving in our car when my cell phone rang. It was our dear friend. She had been to her check up at the hospital in San Antonio, Texas, and had a report for us. She told us that the doctors could not find one single shred of the tumor anywhere in her stomach, and that it was completely gone! They told her that it was a mystery and that it could not be. She told them that it was no mystery, Jesus healed her body and God took that tumor and dissolved it from her body! She has been cancer free and tumor free since that day!

This is an example of laying hands on the sick and them going through the process of recovery. Our friend did not receive a *dunamis* healing. There was no instant miracle that could be measured with the natural eye. The key to her healing was that she received the word of God into her body, soul, and spirit, and she stood strong in her faith to proclaim that God had healed her. When the enemy tried to creep back into her mind and lie to her, she made a phone call and was reminded to keep standing on the promises of God. She stood strong, and God took her through the process of recovery. This is why Jesus said, *"For assuredly, I say to you, if you have faith as a mustard seed, you will say to this mountain, 'Move from here to there,' and it will move; and nothing will be impossible for you"* (Matt. 17:20). Our friend stirred up enough faith to move the tumor from "here to there," and it became possible for her.

Since then, my wife and I have prayed for multitudes of people with cancer. We have seen all but one of them healed from this deadly disease, which is demonic in nature. I cannot explain why one of the persons died while the rest did not. I am not God, but I am not going to let the death of a person stop me from believing that God is still a miracle-working God, who saves, heals, and delivers His people. But I can testify that multitudes of others have been completely made whole, and that brings glory to God! What is important is that you and I continue to grow and walk in our faith so that others might be blessed.

DISILLUSIONED WITH HEALING

I have seen many people become disenchanted with the subject of divine healing from God. I have also found that most of the time, if not all of the time, they lack the necessary revelation to understand the principles of healing that God lays out in scripture. What happens is that someone gets prayed over for a specific healing to occur, and they actually receive the healing—they walk away believing that they have been healed. However, this does not mean that the enemy gives up. The devil and his demonic forces will come creeping back to steal, kill, and destroy. They will come back, lie to that person, and tell them that they weren't really healed, and that person will believe and receive the lie. If you believe the lie, you will receive the lie. Don't get mad at God; it's not God's fault. He already taught us how to believe, how to pray, how to live, and how to resist the devil so that he flees from us.

What happens with some people is that when they still see symptoms of the sickness or disease, they automatically discount the healing and reject it. Doubt and unbelief enter the picture and flood this person's mind with lies about the fact that they did not get healed. Doubt and unbelief are always right. Our job is to eliminate the spirit of doubt and the spirit of unbelief from our lives, not allowing them to speak to us.

Doubt and unbelief are demons; they are unclean spirits. The apostle Paul clearly taught that there are deceiving spirits and doctrines of demons (see 1 Tim. 4:1). Doubt and unbelief are deceiving spirits, whose role is to steal the word of God from the soil of a believer's heart. Just as in the parable of the sower and the seed, it is like the person who received the word on stony places. Although he received the healing with joy, tribulation or symptoms came around, and he stumbled right back into his sickness. The Bible instructs us in the Book of James not to be double minded:

> But let him ask in faith, with no doubting, for he who doubts is like a wave of the sea driven and tossed by the wind. For let not that man suppose that he will receive anything from the Lord; he is a double-minded man, unstable in all his ways (James 1:6-8).

Our job is simply to receive and believe. God's job is to heal instantly, or take us through the process of recovery.

INSTANTANEOUS HEALING

One time I prayed for a friend who was 95 percent deaf in his left ear. During our prayer time for healing, he felt the fire of God come through his ear canal and blow outward from his left ear. He was instantly healed and has complete hearing in his left ear now. This is an example of the dunamis power of God, or an instant miracle.

There is much to be learned about divine healing, and much to be taught about divine healing as I give you one more spiritual "nugget" in reference to healing. Sometimes people don't get healed because they did not get the demon, or unclean spirit, responsible for carrying out the sickness or disease cast out of them first. If you read the Gospels, on many occasions Jesus cast out an unclean spirit and then that person was healed. I have met multitudes of people who have been prayed over, believing for a supernatural healing to occur, but the demons associated with that condition had not been dealt with. Upon dealing with the demons and casting them out of the person, the healing took place in their bodies.

Upon studying the scriptures, you will see that some healings took place with the casting out of demons associated with a process, and some healings took place without casting out any demons. This is a much-needed revelation in the body of Christ today. We must study the scriptures and pray for God to allow us to see them with spiritual eyes. It is the

Holy Spirit who gives us proper interpretation of the scriptures. It is the Holy Spirit who will teach us all things, so we must ask Him to help us. People's lives are hanging in the balances and the application of Jesus's mandate to you and me could save someone's life at any given time.

Either way the healing takes place, God's ministry model works, and it is a joy to experience. The message for you today is: If you believe, you should see healing take place in the lives of the people around you. If you don't believe that divine healing is possible, you don't have to worry about it. God won't bother you with it!

Chapter 10

WAITING AND THIRSTING FOR THE POWER

GREATER WORKS

In John 16 Jesus refers to the fact that it was to our advantage that He would go to the Father, in order that the Helper (the Holy Spirit) might come for us (see John 16:7). We have to keep in mind that Jesus came to *"destroy the works of the devil"* (1 John 3:8). Before He appointed 12 disciples and launched them into the ministry, He was the only power there was. But His promise was that He would send a Helper to equip us with the same anointing that He had to accomplish that for which God sent Him to the earth.

Do you truly feel like you have that same power granted to you to defeat all of the enemies that attack your life? If not, there is a solution, if you will only read on. That's a promise—not from me, but from God! This was exactly why Jesus told His disciples that they would do greater works than He had been doing:

> *Most assuredly, I say to you, he who believes in Me, the works that I do he will do also; and greater works than these he will do, because I go to My Father. And whatever you ask in My name, that I will do, that the Father may be glorified in the Son. If you ask anything in My name, I will do it* (John 14:12-14).

This scripture is directly linked to Jesus talking to His disciples about the keys to the kingdom (see Matt. 16:18-19). When Jesus told Peter that He was giving him the keys to the kingdom, it was a message about the keys of authority. Jesus represents the keys to the kingdom. He tells us that no one gets to the Father except through Him; and the Bible further tells us that He has been granted all authority. Therefore, when we use His name, we are acting with His complete authority. We hold the key to get to the Father's answers. And that key is Jesus. We will do greater works than Jesus performed on earth because He wants us to. His name gives us the same authority He operated in while He was here on earth, so it is like He is with us anyway! In fact, knowing that we have to use His name is a brilliant reminder that we can't do anything without Him. For it is the Bible that tells us that without Him we can do nothing (see John 15:5). But with God, all things are possible!

WAITING FOR POWER

Jesus, in meeting with His remaining 11 disciples, before His ascension to the Father, addressed them with some important instructions. They were to go to Jerusalem and wait for the promise of God. These are believers He was talking to—they have already preached the gospel, healed the sick, and cast out devils by this time. But Jesus was telling them not to depart from Jerusalem, but to wait for a different baptism, the baptism of the Holy Spirit.

And being assembled together with them, He commanded them not to depart from Jerusalem, but to wait for the Promise of the Father, "which," He said, "you have heard from Me; for John truly baptized with water, but you shall be baptized with the Holy Spirit not many days from now" (Acts 1:4-5).

They waited for ten days to get their answer. Can you wait on God for your answer? I have seen many people stretch their hands out, reaching out to God, and asking Him to endue them with power from on high—yet nothing seemed to happen. Most of the time, they leave that setting highly discouraged and begin to doubt that God really does baptize Christians with the Holy Spirit.

I recall a conversation I had in 2001 with a very prominent pastor in one of the largest churches in the United States. Knowing that he was from a traditional Baptist background and a traditional Baptist university, I was delicate about how I approached him in the conversation. As we talked about the power of the Holy Spirit, he told of an account where several of his college buddies had tried to get him to believe in the baptism of the Holy Spirit while in college. He went on to say that they prayed for him but nothing significant happened. I wasn't mature enough in the word of God to have an adequate response to his rejection of this part of God's word, even though I had just received the promise of the Holy Spirit. Even today he is an incredible minister of God, and God works mightily through him. And I still believe that none of us have "arrived." God's anointing comes on him when he preaches, without a doubt. I still adore him and admire him.

But after ten years of experiencing Holy Spirit power in my life and seeing Him work in the lives of other people, I know what I would have said. I would have told him that I don't have all the answers to life's questions. But what I do know is that sometimes you have to be willing to wait upon the Lord. Isaiah said, *"But those who wait on the Lord shall renew their strength; they shall mount up with wings like eagles, they shall run and not be weary, they shall walk and not faint"* (Isa. 40:31). I would have reminded him that just because something didn't happen in his timing did not mean that God was not going to show up in His timing. Sometimes, when you don't get your answer in your timing, you reject the answer totally because you nullify God's timing. I would have also reminded him that the first disciples had to pray and fast for ten days before the Holy Spirit came upon them with cloven tongues of fire! If they had to wait ten days, I believe it is safe to assume that our role is something like this:

- Trust God's word—faith comes by hearing, and hearing by the word of God (see Rom. 10:17).

- By faith, and only by faith, will you receive anything you ask for from the Lord.

- Only believe!

- Be willing to wait upon the Lord, however long it takes.

- Be willing to press in and cry out to God in desperation for the promise of the Holy Spirit.

- Never, ever give up on this promise.

- If you, in your sinful nature, give good gifts to your children, how much more will God give the Holy Spirit to those who ask Him (see Matt. 7:11)?

CONTINUALLY THIRSTY

God's desire is that all Christians walk in the power of the Holy Spirit. Many will say, "I got everything I needed from God when I got saved." As good as this sounds, Paul instructs us to be continually filled with the Holy Spirit (see Eph. 5:18). I prefer to trust God's inspiration and instruction to us via Paul's writings. After you have had a drink from the Holy Spirit, you will want to drink from Him for the rest of your life! This is why the Bible says, *"Oh, taste and see that the Lord is good. Blessed is the man who trusts in Him!"* (Ps. 34:8). And be reminded that Jesus said, *"If anyone thirsts, let him come to Me and drink"* (John 7:37). The key word here is anyone. Anyone can be you! Are you thirsty, or did you get all that you needed on the day that you received salvation?

I can't imagine a person not drinking any water for an extended period of time, such as 100 days or so. Experts say that the maximum amount of days one can live without a drink of water is ten days. These odds have been defied on a few occasions; however, most people could not go more than three to ten days without water. How much more do we need a fresh drink from the Holy Spirit of God? This is exactly why Paul instructs us to be continually filled with the Holy Spirit. This is our spiritual drink that keeps us built up and spiritually healthy.

RECEIVING POWER FROM GOD

The disciples had remembered that Jesus specifically addressed the issue of power, and receiving power. Not only that, but He specifically spoke of the power of the Holy Sprit coming upon them. He said:

*But you shall **receive power** when the Holy Spirit has come **upon** you; and you shall be witnesses to Me in Jerusalem, and in all Judea and Samaria, and to the end of the earth* (Acts 1:8).

There is little to elaborate on concerning this scripture since it is very literal, and it is extremely specific in relation to what is supposed to take place. God desires to endue you with His power. You need Holy Spirit power to be a credible witness to Him in the earth. Peek again at this scripture and notice the word upon. God's power will come upon you if you receive Him by faith.

And then it happened! Just what Jesus foretold, and exactly in the manner in which Jesus said it would, it happened!

*When the Day of Pentecost had fully come, they were all with one accord in one place. And suddenly there came a sound from heaven, as of a rushing mighty wind, and it filled the whole house where they were sitting. Then there appeared to them divided tongues, as of fire, and one sat **upon** each of them. **And they were all filled with the Holy Spirit** and began to speak with other tongues, as the Spirit gave them utterance* (Acts 2:1-4).

This was a post-conversion experience that took place with a group of Christians. The Holy Spirit filled them and endued them with power and fire, just as John the Baptist previously prophesied.

Then Peter was filled with boldness and entered a new dimension of ministry. He said in his sermon to the surrounding people:

> *This Jesus God has raised up, of which we are all witnesses. Therefore being exalted to the right hand of God, and having received from the Father the promise of the Holy Spirit, He poured out this which you now see and hear* (Acts 2:32-33).

Instead of only having courage when he was physically in the presence of Jesus, he now was in the continual presence of the Helper, the Holy Spirit! This enabled him to be the mighty, courageous Peter that spoke with such boldness, not the Peter we read about in the Gospels prior to Jesus's arrest in the Garden of Gethsemane.

SAME ACCESS TO THE POWERFUL HOLY SPIRIT

Here is what I am setting you up for: you are allowed access to the same powerful Spirit that gave Peter this newfound boldness. All you have to do is follow Peter's instructions from the 2nd chapter of Acts.

> *Then Peter said to them, "Repent, and let every one of you be baptized in the name of Jesus Christ for the remission of sins; and you shall receive the gift of the Holy Spirit. For the promise is* **to you** *and* **to your** *children, and* **to**

all *who are afar off,* ***as many*** *as the Lord our God will call"* (Acts 2:38-39).

There are a few key points that we must look at regarding these two pieces of scripture. The real treasure lies in reading the entirety of Acts 2, and you will see that Peter is now preaching with a newfound boldness. Jesus is no longer with him in the flesh, but Jesus is now with him in the Spirit. Because Peter was baptized with the Holy Spirit and with fire, he now had a fresh vision, increased authority, greater revelation, and more boldness than ever before.

Here was Peter, preaching his first sermon, and in front of a multitude of people. He addressed the men of Judea and all who were in Jerusalem. Was this the same guy who denied Jesus three times, and one of those denials to a young girl? Here is how simple receiving the promise of the Holy Spirit is:

- Repent—come clean with any hidden sin, for God already knows. But you need to confess your sins to one another.

- Be baptized—for the remission of sins.

- Receive the gift—receiving the gift of the Holy Spirit (I will expand on this at the end of your journey through this book).

Peter stated that the promise is to you and to your children, and to all who are afar off, as many as the Lord our God will call. Has the Lord God called you? If so, then you are a candidate to receive the same promise that Peter affirmed was available to as many as the Lord our God will call. Peter was making it very clear that the promise is to every generation that followed until the coming of the Lord Jesus. Since Jesus has not come back, all of us who believe are candidates to receive the gift of the Holy Spirit, which is undoubtedly a post-conversion experience.

Chapter 11

BOLDNESS AND OBEDIENCE

NEWFOUND BOLDNESS

After being baptized in the Spirit, Peter and John went out and preached with boldness to the high priests and rulers. Peter was full of boldness as he confronted them with the truth, and it was this very boldness that caused the religious leaders to consider arresting him and John. After conferring with each other, the rulers agreed to let them go instead of arresting them for preaching Jesus. They were so amazed that these "uneducated and untrained" men could speak so profoundly and with such conviction. This is the very reason by which they were not arrested. It was the Holy Spirit, speaking through them, that gave them the boldness to preach with such strength and conviction.

They then went back to their brothers and sisters in Christ and prayed that they would speak with boldness as well. The result was that all were filled with the Holy Spirit and spoke with boldness. Luke writes:

*And when they had prayed, the place where they were assembled together was shaken; and they were **all filled** with the Holy Spirit, and they spoke the word of God with boldness* (Acts 4:31).

If this were a group of believers that had already received the promise of the Holy Spirit, then the passage merely supports the apostle Paul's teaching of being continually filled with the Holy Spirit. It is a strong message to all of us as Christians, to not be satisfied with operating from yesterday's anointing. Jesus even addressed this when He referred to pouring new wine into old wineskins, and the inability of the old wineskin to hold the new wine (see Matt. 9:16-17). If we want something new from Jesus and a fresh infilling of the Holy Spirit, sometimes we must shed some of the old beliefs we have fostered. They are analogous to old, cracked wineskins that cannot handle new wine (new revelation). That old belief system doesn't give you the capacity to understand what the Holy Spirit has in store for you, much less be able to handle it. Pray to God to be filled with the Holy Spirit and to speak with boldness!

TO THOSE WHO OBEY HIM

And we are His witnesses to these things, and so also is the Holy Spirit whom God has given to those who obey Him (Acts 5:32).

Once again, here is the "new" Peter, addressing the religious leaders of the day. The important issue I want to point out here is not necessarily that Peter is addressing religious leaders, but that he is revealing to whom the Holy Spirit is given. God has given the Holy Spirit to those who obey Him. Do you obey Him?

I have seen a lot of people come before God to receive the power of the Holy Spirit and not receive Him. I do not have all of the answers on this subject. But if the disciples had to wait for ten days before receiving the promise of the Spirit, then I guess some of us might have to wait more than ten seconds after we ask. I know that I had to wait five days after the truth of the gift of the Holy Spirit was shown to me. For me, there was a disobedience issue that needed to be cleared up, one that only God knew about. But God knew, therefore, I was unable to receive from Him what I wanted. I didn't even know about this scripture at the time—it just validates how my waiting experience of five days had to take place. Once I got my issue cleared up and confessed my sin, the Holy Spirit consumed me with fire.

You see, I was desperate for God and I was desperate for change. And because I was desperate for righteousness, God brought me under heavy conviction of every hidden sin that I had in my life during those 13 years of rebellion before He would grant me the promise that He gives only to those who obey Him. The Bible says, *"For there is nothing hidden which will not be revealed, nor has anything been kept secret but that it should come to light"* (Mark 4:22).

Some people might say, "That sure sounds legalistic!" But I say that it is the word of God, and that God is a God of justice. It's not about jumping through a bunch of hoops, like some would declare. It is really about being desperate to live a righteous and holy life, and watching God show up in the midst of it. The Holy Spirit is not a piece of trick-or-treat candy that we can just knock on the door and ask for regardless of what costume we are wearing. He is a real person—He is God, in Spirit. He knows what lies behind the mask and costume. He knows everyone's heart, He knows exactly where we are in life, and He knows exactly what He is willing to give us according to the principles in which He established.

DEPENDING ON GOD'S WORD

Stephen, who was martyred shortly into his ministry, made it clear to the religious leaders that they were resistant to change. He said, *"You stiff-necked and uncircumcised in heart and ears! You always resist the Holy Spirit; as your fathers did, so do you"* (Acts 7:51).

He was addressing devout Jews when he said this. In other words, these were men who professed to love God with all of their hearts, they thought that they had all of the truth, that their fathers had taught them well, and they lived their life according to sound doctrine. They were grounded, or so they thought, and they didn't need anybody coming into their "camp" and telling them that God may have more for them than what they already knew. Hosea declared:

My people are destroyed for lack of knowledge. Because you have rejected knowledge, I also will reject you from being priest for Me; because you have forgotten the law of your God, I also will forget your children (Hosea 4:6).

It is always the religious people who attack other Christians on fire for God. When you see a Christian on fire for God, the unsaved are drawn to them. The unsaved are curious, impressed, and want to know more as to why the Christian is so on fire. But the religious Christian brothers, those who have all of the answers from their doctrines of men and have their whole system in place want to wipe out any threat of another Christian being on fire for God. How dare someone be so bold as to preach the word of God with boldness, authority, and conviction? Most religious people that I have seen say it something like this: "Can you believe how off-track he is?" Or they say, "You just need to get some balance in your life." Sometimes you can be referred to as a "Jesus freak." The definition of a Jesus freak is someone who loves Jesus a little more than you do! So watch out for who you call a Jesus freak!

The real message here is not to count on your fathers for the absolute truth. Count on the word of God for your truth. Fathers and mentors always have the human ability to fail, and to fail you—they are not always right. But the word of God is always right. I do believe in wise counsel, mentors, and fathers in the Lord, so don't take this as black and white. I am a firm believer in accountability, teaching everywhere I go about the vital importance of being connected to two or three sound, equally-yoked, accountability partners. I have accountability partners and I have two fathers in the Lord, in whom I have great trust. Sometimes, because of our humanity, we just put men and systems created by men in a higher place than God. And whatever we have put in a higher place than God becomes an idol, creating the possibility for us to miss the truth because of the pride and spiritual blindness that can accompany any idolatrous issue. It is time we depend on God's word and take Him out of our man-made box.

Chapter 12

TAKE GOD OUT OF THE BOX

A POST-CONVERSION EXPERIENCE

Now when the apostles who were at Jerusalem heard that Samaria had received the word of God, they sent Peter and John to them, who, when they had come down, prayed for them that they might receive the Holy Spirit. For as yet He had fallen upon none of them. They had only been baptized in the name of the Lord Jesus. Then they laid hands on them, and they received the Holy Spirit (Acts 8:14-17).

Here is the outline of the above passage:

- When they believed

- They were baptized

- And the Holy Spirit had yet to fall on any of them

I mentioned earlier that the Gospels were written to bring us into the knowledge and belief in Jesus Christ, which leads to salvation, healing, and deliverance. The Book of Acts is positioned right after the Gospels on purpose. It was not an accident that Acts follows the Gospels instead of being placed after Ephesians. The Book of Acts is validation of everything in which John the Baptist and Jesus foretold would happen concerning the Holy Spirit and fire coming upon believers.

It is very apparent through reading these particular scriptures that the power of the Holy Spirit coming upon a believer is an essential post-conversion experience that every person who believes should yearn for. If the new believers in Samaria had simply become believers and been baptized in water, it seems as if they might have received all they needed. They could have easily said, "Hey, we got everything we needed the day we got saved." But this was not the case. The apostles sent Peter and John to pray for them that they might receive the Holy Spirit! This is a post-conversion experience.

The above scripture is yet another story, another testimony, of what happens when believers get a revelation that God has more for them after they initially receive the word and are baptized. As evidenced in chapter 8 of Acts, the Holy Spirit had not fallen upon the believers in Samaria, that is, until Peter and John laid hands on them—then they received.

WHAT'S FIRST?

You may be wondering, "Why doesn't someone receive the promise of the Holy Spirit immediately after being born again and baptized in water?" It is because we cannot limit God, though I'm sure we have tried to limit Him many times.

I recall a time when a young college student from Texas A&M University was at a large coliseum worship service where a popular Christian artist was performing, which I was also at. After the service was over, he came to me, looked me in the eye, and asked, "How do I get right with God, because I need to get right with God?"

I asked him how much he knew about Jesus and quickly found out that he knew very little about Him and had no clue who Peter was! I took him through some scriptures and explained to him what being saved really meant—explaining that the Greek word for "saved" was sozo, which also meant healing and deliverance. I explained that when he gave his life to Christ, he was going to be delivered from all his demons, that he would be healed anywhere in his body that might need healing, and that he was going to be born again—saved. I led him through a prayer as he accepted Christ as his Lord and Savior, and he was transformed.

I then told him that God wanted to come upon him with power and fire, and give him the promise of the

Holy Spirit. He was excited to know there was more! As I laid my hands gently on his chest, the Holy Spirit of God took total control of this young man's body and engulfed him with power and fire from heaven. He laid on the floor in a room for about 30 minutes, basking in the glory of God, in another state of being. His spirit was communing with the Holy Spirit and he did not care about anything else in the world. Take note that this young man was receiving Holy Spirit power, but he had yet to be baptized in water.

Acts 10 confirms something similar:

While Peter was still speaking these words, the Holy Spirit fell upon all those who heard the word. And those of the circumcision who believed were astonished, as many as came with Peter, because the gift of the Holy Spirit had been poured out on the Gentiles also. For they heard them speak with tongues and magnify God.

Then Peter answered, "Can anyone forbid water, that these should not be baptized who have received the Holy Spirit just as we have?" And he commanded them to be baptized in the name of the Lord. Then they asked him to stay a few days (Acts 10:44-48).

Here is another validation of the post-conversion experience of the Holy Spirit falling upon believers. Remember, you must ask yourself, "Am I a believer?"

If you answered yes to that question, then that means the Holy Spirit is available to come into your life with power from on high, to come upon you, and to fill you will with rivers of living water that will flow from your heart.

The other key point in this verse is in regards to water baptism occurring *after* these people received the power of the Holy Spirit. I believe this account is in the Bible to keep us from restricting God to one particular method or system. Just as the thief on the cross met Jesus in paradise without being baptized in water, these new believers received the Holy Spirit and spoke in tongues before they were ever physically immersed in water. The message is to not limit God and how He wants to do something in someone's life. That's why we never put God in a "box." He ultimately will do anything He wants to do, anytime He wants to do it, and however He wishes to perform it!

At the time, I did not know a whole lot about this young college student from Texas A&M. What I found out over the next few days caused me to jump for joy. I found out that he drove back to College Station, Texas, went to the bar in which he worked as a bartender, and quit his job! He told his boss that he could not work at a bar anymore. He found a church in College Station that supported him. He developed a relationship very quickly with the pastor and the pastor's son, and became a solid disciple of Christ.

I pray that he is still serving the Lord with all of his heart even today.

When you deal with people who come to know Christ, and do not have a religious background, there is no telling how quickly God can begin to work in their life. Most of the time, their spirit is willing to receive all that God has for them because it has not been cluttered with religious lies and deceptions planted by the enemy through the means of false doctrines or doctrines of demons.

SAUL BECOMES PAUL: A POST-CONVERSION EXPERIENCE

And Ananias went his way and entered the house; and laying his hands on him he said, "Brother Saul, the Lord Jesus, who appeared to you on the road as you came, has sent me that you may receive your sight and be filled with the Holy Spirit." Immediately there fell from his eyes something like scales, and he received his sight at once; and he arose and was baptized (Acts 9:17-18).

Here comes yet another validation of the post-conversion experience that you may have never had, but it is available to you just as it was to Saul of Tarsus. Saul, whom we all know, was a devout Jewish leader, a religious scholar, and a faithful persecutor of all men who professed that Jesus Christ was the Messiah. While on his way to Damascus to persecute more

Christians, Jesus showed up in a powerful light and spoke to him. Saul not only fell to the ground but also confessed Jesus as Lord. He asked Jesus, "Lord, what do You want me to do?" However, this new convert was blinded for three days and had yet to be baptized in water, but God had a post-conversion plan for him. God sent a faithful Christian named Ananias to lay hands on him so that he would receive his sight and be filled with the Holy Spirit.

I don't understand how some wonderful Christian people out there can say they got everything God had for them at the time of their salvation experience. I would never limit God to think that this could not happen to someone all at once, but not in the frequency in which I hear this weak response to the revelation of the Holy Spirit and fire. It is a weak and prideful way of saying, "That's hogwash, and you can't teach me anything that I don't already know." The sad part is that you rarely hear this kind of response from a person who bears good fruit. These are the kind of statements you hear from someone who dresses nice on Sundays, puts on a big smile, and puts their $20 bill in the offering each service.

But behind the scenes and beneath the surface there are hidden problems, moods, and behaviors that aren't pleasing to God in those same people's lives. There are actually many other possibilities other than this, but it would take an entire book to address this particular subject alone.

THE SAME ANOINTING UPON YOU

As Peter preached, he said, *"God anointed Jesus of Nazareth with the Holy Spirit and with power, who went about doing good and healing all who were oppressed by the devil, for God was with Him"* (Acts 10:38).

Jesus foretold of all that was to come, and now Peter was giving an account of what happened. This is the same message we are to adhere to today. Jesus foretold and we give an account of all that He said and all that He promised. Since Jesus told us that we were to do greater works than Him using His name, it would seem necessary that we would need the same kind of anointing from God that Jesus received. In the scripture above, God anointed Jesus with the Holy Spirit and with power. This anointing allowed Him to do good works, which were demonstrated by power, and heal people who were oppressed by the devil. Here is the result of you seeking God for an anointing of the Holy Spirit:

- You will be a vessel for God's power.

- You will be able to do good works.

- You will be able to heal people who are oppressed by the devil.

- And you will be able to do all this because God is with you, in Spirit.

THE HOLY SPIRIT FELL UPON THE GENTILES

Again, Peter said in addressing the rest of the disciples after the Holy Spirit had been poured out on the Gentiles:

*And as I began to speak, the Holy Spirit fell **upon** them, as upon us at the beginning. Then I remembered the word of the Lord, how He said, "John indeed baptized with water, but you shall be baptized with the Holy Spirit." If therefore God gave them the same gift as He gave us when we believed on the Lord Jesus Christ, who was I that I could withstand God?* (Acts 11:15-17)

As you read Acts chapter 11 on your own, you will become familiar with Peter's story of being obedient to God, ministering where the Holy Spirit sent him, regardless of what human wisdom might think. His obedience led to another powerful testimony of the Holy Spirit falling upon new believers. The key message Peter was trying to get across was *that it happened to them just like it happened to us.* It should happen to you, too, just like it happened for my wife, my children, and me, if you only believe.

The experience or process doesn't always happen the same way for every person. In this case, Peter was preaching the word of God and the Holy Spirit began to fall upon the believers. He was not laying hands on anyone. There was no prayer line. He wasn't pushing someone over and trying to knock him or her to the ground as being "slain in the Spirit." He was merely preaching the word of God when the Holy Spirit took over. Peter's humility and wisdom allowed him to see that he was in a situation where he just needed to let the Holy Spirit take over and perform the work in which He intended. Peter had a great attitude in that he asked, *"Who was I that I could withstand God?"* (Acts 11:17).

If you have an attitude of expectancy, you will be surprised by the many different ways in which people receive the promise of the Holy Spirit. I have listened to tapes and CDs of people who received the power of the Holy Spirit while they were driving in their car, and they had to pull over to the side of the road because of the experience. I have heard stories of people receiving the power of the Holy Spirit in their prayer time, while spending quiet time with God.

I had a close friend crawl out of bed and stand up in his bedroom because he was watching a Joyce Meyer teaching on the Holy Spirit. Joyce Meyer instructed the crowd to stand up, reach their arms out to God, and prepare to receive the promise of the Holy Spirit if they were ready. My friend crawled out of bed and his wife asked, "What in the world are you doing?"

He said, "I'm about to receive the Holy Spirit!" As soon as he spoke those words and extended his arms to God, the Holy Spirit totally immersed him in power and fire! He was in a supernatural state with

God for about three hours. His wife did not quite know what to think, but a few days later we prayed for her to receive the Holy Spirit, and she received Him as well!

These few examples are meant to encourage you to prepare yourself for any move of the Holy Spirit that takes place. That's why God said, *"For My thoughts are not your thoughts, nor are your ways My ways…"* (Isa. 55:8). Don't ever limit God sending the promise of the Holy Spirit to you or anyone else by various means. If you prepare yourself, and prepare others to maintain an attitude of expectancy, you will see a lot of happy people enjoy the power of God. Our role is to continue to encourage people with the word for the sole purpose of them developing their faith. The word of God is what comes alive in someone's body, soul, and spirit. It is the word of God, and only the word of God can create the belief, the faith, and the expectancy that God's promises are not empty promises. If He says that He will baptize you with the Holy Spirit and with fire, then He will do it. You just have to hold up your end of the bargain—only believe!

Chapter 13

POWER RELEASES GIFTS

RECEIVING THE HOLY SPIRIT WHEN BELIEVING

*And it happened, while Apollos was at Corinth, that Paul, having passed through the upper regions, came to Ephesus. And finding some disciples he said to them, **"Did you receive the Holy Spirit when you believed?"***

So they said to him, "We have not so much as heard whether there is a Holy Spirit."

And he said to them, "Into what then were you baptized?"

So they said, "Into John's baptism."

Then Paul said, "John indeed baptized with a baptism of repentance, saying to the people that they should believe on Him who would come after him, that is, on Christ Jesus."

*When they heard this, they were baptized in the name of the Lord Jesus. And when Paul had laid hands on them, the Holy Spirit came **upon** them, and they spoke with tongues and prophesied. Now the men were about twelve in all* (Acts 19:1-7).

This is one of the key verses in Acts regarding the power of the Holy Spirit. When Paul traveled to Ephesus, he found 12 disciples there. We must take note that 12 disciples means 12 believers. So the first question that Paul had for this group of believers was, "Did you receive the Holy Spirit when you believed?" This is a very profound statement.

Here were a group of followers of Christ who had not even heard of the Holy Spirit. It kind of reminds me of what happened to me at age 35. I had heard the words "Holy Spirit" many times in my life, but had never been asked if I had received the Holy Spirit when I believed. Obviously, we see that the outcome is yet another validation that there is a definite post-conversion experience that we as believers have available to us.

Paul was not afraid to ask this question because he knew how important receiving the Holy Spirit was to any believer. It was his knowledge and understanding that only the Holy Spirit would release spiritual gifts into one's life for the work of the ministry and for the edification of the body of Christ (the church). As evidenced here, we see that these particular believers immediately spoke in tongues and prophesied.

TONGUES AS INITIAL EVIDENCE?

I spoke in tongues two weeks after I received the power of the Holy Spirit. Much of the time, people get taught in Pentecostal or Charismatic circles that the evidence of one receiving the promise of the Holy Spirit is speaking in tongues. For example, a minister might ask, "Did you receive the baptism of the Holy Spirit with the evidence of speaking in tongues?" This is not necessarily accurate. One can certainly speak in tongues immediately upon receiving the promise of the Holy Spirit. However, it is not mandatory.

I had an unbelievable power encounter with the Holy Spirit of God when I received the promise of the Spirit. I got up off the ground that night, went home, and woke up the next morning with a purpose of ministering to others who were in need of freedom from demonic oppressions or who needed healing. I witnessed miracles all around me, yet I did not speak in tongues for at least two weeks. Then one day, in my prayer closet, I began uttering unknown words to God. Thus, I began speaking in tongues. The reason this happened is because I eagerly desired for God to release that gift in me. I had been crying out for God to let me speak in tongues so that I could utter mysteries to Him. I had been digesting the word and reading everything I could about tongues and the purposes for it. Because of this, my faith was increasing more and more each day to step out and let God loosen my tongue and speak in an unknown language. And it happened!

I have ministered to countless numbers of people who received the promise of the Holy Spirit upon being prayed for but did not immediately speak in an unknown tongue. I have also ministered to several people who began praying in tongues before my hands ever reached their body to lay hands on them to receive the promise of the Holy Spirit. And I have ministered to many people who began speaking in tongues immediately upon receiving the promise of the Holy Spirit. We just can't limit God on how the timing of things is going to work out with each individual. You and I have one major role, and that is to trust God's word. Only believe!

RELEASING PROPHECY

Prior to receiving the Holy Spirit at the age of 35, I had never prophesied over anybody's life. In fact, I really did not have a clue what prophecy was! The moment I received the power of God, there was an immediate shift in my ability to perceive spiritual matters. Sometimes God would just show me someone's past experiences, or their present situation, and give me a word of encouragement and specific scriptures to build their faith in order to keep them focused on their destiny in Christ Jesus. Prophecy is simply being able to see part of someone's past, their present situation, and where they are going. All of this, of course, is in part because we are not able to see every aspect of someone's past, present, and future. The Bible says that we know in part, and that we prophesy in part (see 1 Cor. 13:9). Prophecy is for the building up and edification of the church (see 1 Cor. 14:3). It is used to reach people and encourage them. There is much to say about prophecy, however, I will not go into great detail here.

God still allows me to do this today, but I know that I can't speak encouraging words like that to people without the power and direction that only comes from the Holy Spirit of God. I also know that this gift came as a result of the Holy Spirit falling upon me, and it will continue to remain in my life until I die or until Jesus comes back, whichever happens first. This is clearly stated by Paul the apostle (see 1 Cor. 13:10).

IMPORTANCE OF BEING INTRODUCED TO THE HOLY SPIRIT

Paul was very adamant about asking the question, *"Did you receive the Holy Spirit when you believed?"* (Acts 19:2). He was going to make sure that he did his job as a steward of the word of God, to equip the saints for the work of the ministry (see Eph. 4:11-16). Paul knew that he wasn't Jesus and that he could only do so much. Like Paul, when we recognize that we are only one person, we develop a clearer understanding of how important it is to introduce people to the Holy Spirit. And when I speak of introducing people to the Holy Spirit, I am talking about introducing them to Him in such a way that goes far beyond mere head knowledge. So many Christians just know the Holy

Spirit as being the third part of the Trinity. They merely recognize the Holy Spirit as God in Spirit. They have not been introduced to the Holy Spirit as the Comforter, the Helper, or as their perfect ministry partner. My question to you would be the same as Paul's. In fact, this is the question I am just now beginning to understand that I need to be asking fellow believers on a more consistent basis: "How do you know if you have received the Holy Spirit?"

HOW TO KNOW IF YOU'VE RECEIVED THE SPIRIT

First of all, you will just know. The Holy Spirit manifests Himself in someone's life according to how He chooses. Not everyone feels lightning bolts coming through their hands like I did. I have seen far greater manifestations of His power than I have ever experienced myself. I have heard many different responses from believers who have received the power of the Holy Spirit described as such:

- I felt like I was completely underwater.

- I felt like it was raining on my head, and pouring down my body.

- I felt my fingers and toes tingling the whole time.

- I felt like warm honey was being poured all over my head.

- I felt like a million volts of electricity were going through my body.

- I felt like I was drinking water and couldn't stop.

- I felt like I was just floating.

And there are many more than these. However, I just wanted to give you an example of the reality of God. He will not be put into a box. He shows up how He wants to show up and when He wants to show up. I give you some of these real-life examples to encourage you, and to make sure you don't have a certain way that you expect God to manifest His presence in your life. Our only job when desiring to receive the Holy Spirit is to be expectant. The rest is up to God.

Secondly, you will know you received the Holy Spirit because of the manifestation of spiritual gifts that begin to become evident in your life as a result of Him coming upon you and filling you. The manifestations of the nine spiritual gifts are listed in First Corinthians 12:4-11:

> There are diversities of gifts, but the same Spirit (Holy Spirit). There are differences of ministries, but the same Lord. And there are diversities of activities, but it is the same God who works all in all. But the manifestation of the Spirit is given to each one for the profit of all: for to one is given the **word of wisdom** through the Spirit,

*to another the **word of knowledge** through the same Spirit, to another **faith** by the same Spirit, to another **gifts of healings** by the same Spirit, to another the **working of miracles**, to another **prophecy**, to another **discerning of spirits**, to another **different kinds of tongues**, to another the **interpretation of tongues**. But one and the same Spirit works all these things, distributing to each one individually as He wills.*

A FEW WORDS ABOUT GIFTS

I want to briefly say a few things about these gifts so that you have an idea of what to expect from God once you receive His promise. When I received the Holy Spirit, I immediately began to see things and understand things from a supernatural standpoint that I had never seen or understood before. These things were very clear to me, but I had not yet learned about the nine types of manifestations of the Holy Spirit in a believer's life. It is evident to me now, from experience and from the word of God, that a believer can operate in any range of these giftings, from one gift to all of the gifts. Personally, I have been fortunate enough to have witnessed all nine of these manifestations of the Spirit occur in my life since I received the promise of the Holy Spirit. Some of these gifts have been used much more than others.

When I first received the promise of the Holy Spirit, I purchased a series of books on the gifts of the Spirit and read everything I could get my hands on about spiritual gifts. I wanted to understand these gifts and how God wanted to use me as a vessel for Him with these different gifts. The most important lesson you should always remember is that it's all about God, not *our* gifts. The manifestation gifts of the Holy Spirit are for the purpose of building up and edifying people, for the sole purpose of pointing them toward their destiny in Christ. In other words, these gifts are for the purpose of directing people's hearts and minds toward the King. God gets 100 percent of the glory, and we should be excited and humbled that He will use us as a vessel to reach people with these gifts. The proper use of them will help build His church.

When it comes to the spiritual gifts Paul speaks of, think about going to war without any weapons. Would it make any sense to go out to the battlefield and begin fighting, yet not have any real weapons? You would be restricted to accomplishing your objective in your own strength. This is what it's like on the battlefield of life, when you go out into the world ready to represent the Lord Jesus Christ in an effort to win souls. You wind up trying to battle the enemy in your own strength. The Bible says:

> For the weapons of our warfare are not carnal but mighty in God for pulling down strongholds, casting down arguments and every high thing that exalts itself against the knowledge of God, bringing every thought into captivity to the obedience of Christ, and being ready to

punish all disobedience when your obedience is fulfilled (2 Corinthians 10:4-6).

We do not have carnal weapons. But we do have the word of God, and I would never want to discount that. For some Christians, this is their main weapon because it is their only weapon. Although the Bible is the most powerful weapon in a Christian's arsenal, it can't be the only weapon if one is looking to fulfill all that God has called them to fulfill on this earth.

Jesus said, *"But the hour is coming, and now is, when the true worshipers will worship the Father in spirit and truth; for the Father is seeking such to worship Him"* (John 4:23). This is exactly why the promise of the Holy Spirit is so vital to your life as a believer. The Bible says that true worshipers won't just go out and try to win souls with a Bible in hand. The most effective Christians will be those who minister to the hearts and minds of people with truth (the Bible) and in Spirit (the Helper). This is precisely where the nine manifestation gifts of the Holy Spirit come into play in a believer's life. They are to help you and me become more effective in carrying out the Great Commission by utilizing both spirit and truth.

Chapter 14

THE MANIFESTATION GIFTS OF THE SPIRIT

GENERAL UNDERSTANDING OF THE GIFTS' FUNCTION

Before I begin with shedding some light on the nine manifestation gifts of the Spirit, I want you to know that entire books can be found on the subject of spiritual gifts. In fact, entire books can be found on each of these gifts individually. There is so much to say about each one of the gifts and there is so much Scriptural evidence to support the function of these gifts, but my purpose here, in this chapter and those following, is to give you a brief synopsis of each gift. I am going to leave it up to you to continue to read the word of God, read anointed books, pray, and study this subject on your own. The reason for this is that I want you to have a general understanding of their function so that you have a better understanding as to why all believers need Holy Spirit power in their lives. I have witnessed a lot of people that receive the promise of the Holy Spirit, yet do not know what the whole purpose for having the Holy Spirit is. The nine manifestation gifts of the Holy Spirit of God are part of the equation in this whole process.

WORD OF WISDOM

The first gift of the Holy Spirit is the word of wisdom. By definition, wisdom means "the quality or state of being wise; knowledge of what is true or right coupled with just judgment as to action; sagacity, discernment, or insight."[1] A word of wisdom is when the Holy Spirit gives a supernatural piece of wisdom that is administered to someone for the purpose of meeting a specific need in his or her life.

For example, you may be having a conversation with someone, and for some reason you have an urgency to share an insight with them about a specific issue that has the appearance of coming out of "nowhere." It flows out of your mouth very easily, and it may not even sound that profound to you because you are just having a conversation. On the other hand, the party to whom you are speaking with has been struggling with answers on how to deal with that exact issue, and you did not even know about it. They got their answer through a word of wisdom, as given by the Holy Spirit, because they had been praying and looking for a concrete answer to their dilemma. God happened to have used you as a vessel to encourage them.

Another way that a word of wisdom can manifest is by offering wisdom to others when they are actually seeking advice. Some believers, in whom God has released a significant measure of this gift, do very well in serving the Lord through relationships. Believers, who use this gift humbly and with temperance, are able to administer extraordinary wisdom and advice to others in times of need. Many times, the believer doesn't feel like they have anything extraordinary to say. They are merely being obedient and speaking to others in love. But the manifestation of the Holy Spirit shows up in the form of a word of wisdom for the other person.

To the person who receives, they perceive the advice as extraordinary. Often, you will hear a response from someone later such as, "The other day, when you were telling me all about how you improved your relationship with your parents, you don't even realize what an impact that has made on my life already. It was like God was speaking to me through you, and it was exactly what I was supposed to hear. Here is what has happened..." Prior to this, however, you may not have even known that there was a problem with their relationship with their parents. A word of wisdom can occur in either type of setting. Remember, God can do whatever He wants, whenever He wants!

WORD OF KNOWLEDGE

A word of knowledge is a supernaturally inspired piece of information that the Lord gives you, usually concerning someone's life. I believe the purpose for a word of knowledge is for the Lord to give you, by supernatural means, a fact about someone's life in order to get their attention.

The first experience I ever had with words of knowledge occurred at my home in early 2001. I had a newfound friend who had a lot of experience with spiritual gifts, especially the gift of prophecy. One night, he was at my home teaching two of my friends and me about how to listen to the voice of God. We were all young in our Spirit-filled walk, and we wanted so badly to see the gifts of the Spirit operate in our lives. Our mentor friend told us that he was going to teach us how to receive a word of knowledge from the Lord. He was going to put some worship music on, and we were all going to pray for a few minutes and ask God to give us a word of knowledge for him (the mentor). He further told us that a word of knowledge could be a word, a sentence, a symbol, a picture, or any type of communication that God put into our spirit.

During this few short minutes, which seemed like eternity, all I could picture was a dozen red roses. This picture would not leave my mind! When our friend stopped praying and asked us each what God showed us, I knew that I didn't have anything to offer. I was the last guy out of three to give my word of knowledge, and I told my mentor friend that I didn't really have anything because mine was silly. He pressed me to tell him what God showed me, no matter how silly it seemed. I told him that all I could see was a dozen red roses. He knew exactly what that meant. He was supposed to buy his wife a dozen red roses that day, and he didn't do it! It was a supernatural piece of information that both him and the Lord knew.

At another time I was meeting with a man who was seeking counsel from me because he was in financial turmoil. At the time we were living in Tennessee, and so was this man. We had known each other for about five months, but I did not know much about him because we did not have any kind of close relationship. As he was sharing all of his financial woes with me, I could not keep my eyes off of a ring he was wearing that displayed a weird symbol.

As he continued to talk, the Holy Spirit began showing me a picture in my mind that was as clear as watching a movie screen about an incident in this man's life. At that point, I knew the Holy Spirit wanted me to interrupt and do the talking. So I asked the man, "Can I ask you a question?"

The answer was, "Yes."

I asked, "At one point and time in your life, were you flying over the piney woods of east Texas in a small plane...and did that plane lose its power... and did you start skimming over the tops of the trees thinking that your life was about to end...but at the last second...the propeller kicked in again...you regained control and landed safely: did anything like this happen?"

This man, who was about 62 years old, almost came out of his chair! His eyes got as big as golf balls, and he asked me, "How did you know that? Nobody knows about that!"

I told him, "Sir, God knows about that because He wants you to know that it was Him who allowed your engine to kick in again, and that He saved you from that death. Now the Lord wants me to tell you something..." And I went on to share more of what God wanted me to tell him.

You see, the Holy Spirit had given me a word of knowledge for this man, a fact about his life, so that I could minister to him and help him. A word of knowledge is for the purpose of building up or edifying another's life, which will lead to building up His church.

But the story did not end there. The Lord gave me that word of knowledge because God wanted to get that man's attention so that he would know that He was there, and that He wanted to draw the man closer toward Him.

God clearly showed me the man's ring had a demonic symbol on it, and it had brought a curse upon his life. I asked him where he had gotten the ring. He said it was a ring he had gotten when he joined the Masonic Lodge in 1993. I asked him this question: "How many heart attacks have you had?"

He replied, "Several."

I asked him when his first heart attack occurred, and he told me that it was in 1993. I went on to tell him that his heart attacks began as a result of the curse upon his life for joining that organization, which was in rebellion toward God, when he placed the ring on his finger. I told him that God wanted him to repent for joining that organization, wanted him to throw the ring away, and He wanted to have a personal relationship with him. I told him that the answers to his problems began right there. Amazingly, the man replied with a bunch of lip service and head nodding, but his heart was not into changing. The Bible reminds us: *"These people draw near to Me with their mouth, and honor Me with their lips, but their heart is far from Me"* (Matt. 15:8).

This example shows how we, as humans, have the power of choice. We can choose to believe God and obey Him, or we can choose to believe our own selfish hearts and live with the consequences. You would think that anybody in their right mind, who heard a word of knowledge about their life such as this one, would be falling on their face before God, begging for His forgiveness. You would think that they would commit their life to Christ right there on the spot, and commit to serve Him faithfully the rest of their lives. Normally, this would hold true; however, there are exceptions to the norm. That is why there is still evil in this world. The devil has a stronghold on some people's lives, and God wants to use supernatural means to get their attention and get through to them. Sometimes, we see that they have ears to hear, but they do not hear. You just have to keep pressing on, sowing seeds that benefit others, and serving the Lord.

Here are the facts: Even though this man did not truly respond to God's call upon his life, he did acknowledge that what I had to say was from God. He knew that God was trying to get his attention. He just could not muster up enough faith to change. Think about me telling this guy those same things about his ring, his heart attacks, and his involvement with a cult organization he was a member of without preceding it with a word of knowledge from the Lord. He would have thought I was mad! He would have thought that I was some whacked out, judgmental, Bible-thumping fanatic who acted like everybody was going to hell except me!

This is where the Holy Spirit can help you become much more loving and effective in ministering to the needs of others. A word of knowledge can be powerfully encouraging. As you learn more about this gift, you will learn that the word of knowledge will always lead to what the Lord wants to say to that person next. It's almost like God saying, "OK, now that I have your undivided attention, here is what I want you to know."

NOTE

1. "Wisdom." Dictionary.com. Dictionary.com Unabridged. Random House, Inc. http://dictionary.reference.com/browse/wisdom (accessed: March 18, 2012).

Chapter 15

FAITH AND HEALING

THE GIFT OF FAITH

The gift of faith certainly relates to faith. *Faith* is defined as the *"substance of things hoped for, the evidence of things not seen"* (Heb. 11:1). Although you haven't seen it, faith is what fuels the hope that you will see the finish line in every area of your hopes and dreams. Faith is the perpetual fuel that feeds mankind. We all need faith to fuel us. The gift of faith is a supernatural impartation of faith itself, which is brought forth by the Holy Spirit.

There are, however, measures of faith. Paul said, *"For I say, through the grace given to me, to everyone who is among you, not to think of himself more highly than he ought to think, but to think soberly, as God has dealt to each one a **measure** of faith"* (Rom. 12:3). Each one of us has been given a certain measure of faith, which is clearly described here. Paul is urging believers not to get prideful and think too highly of themselves because they seem to have more faith than the next guy. But some people simply do have a measure of faith that sometimes appears that they believe they can pull off anything.

This is where the need for the gift of faith comes into all of our lives. When we receive the promise and power of the Holy Spirit, He can bring forth the faith in us to pray for a sick person, or to believe for a miracle or for a trial to be overcome. It is the supernatural gift of faith that can rise up in Spirit-filled believers that actually causes them to believe that *"I can do all things through Christ who strengthens me"* (Phil. 4:13). This is undoubtedly one of the most commonly quoted scriptures in the entire Bible. How many times have you heard, "My favorite verse in the Bible is *'I can do all things through Christ who strengthens me'*?" We would all be millionaires if we had a dollar for every time we heard someone say something like this.

But do all of those people really, deep down, believe that they can do "all things" through Christ? The answer would be a whole lot different with a bunch of believers who have received the promise of the Holy Spirit and have been able to witness the gift of faith being brought forth by way of the Holy Spirit. I know that I want to see this gift working throughout my life because I need the Helper to increase my faith. How about you?

GIFTS OF HEALINGS

The spiritual gifts of healings seems to be specifically related to supernaturally ministering healing to someone in need. Remember that there are two general processes related to the receiving of healing by an individual. One is the dunamis (dynamite) power of God, in which someone receives an instant healing. The other is the process of healing, which entails the laying on of hands and the sick going through the process of recovery. Either way, the gift of healings occurs supernaturally, due to the fact that the Holy Spirit is the one who is administering the healing. Because spiritual gifts are a manifestation of the Spirit, God will use us as a vessel to minister healing to His people. The gifts of healings are pretty simple from a theological standpoint:

- God heals.

- So He uses people as vessels, thus creating a definite need to receive His power from on high.

- We use the name of Jesus.

- The Holy Spirit manifests, or comes forth, and does His work.

I'll never forget what kind of urgency I had to pray for the sick immediately after I received the promise of the Holy Spirit. Prior to that day in 2001, I never had a strong desire to pray for sick people, nor did I really have the faith to. But our house became very busy during those first few months. When people started getting healed, they started talking, and the next thing we knew was that people, who wanted to be made well, were calling and coming from all directions. When you begin to minister to the sick, your eyes open up to how many people there really are around you who have ailments of all varieties. Your eyes also open up to how many people believe God doesn't heal anymore. They are real good at attacking you, and they give credit to God for the attack because they want to be "faithful" ambassadors of God's word.

Personally, I have seen hundreds of people supernaturally healed, and many people saved from premature death as a result. Jesus, the ultimate Healer, got mocked, persecuted, and suffered railing accusations as a result of His good works. With that being the case, you and I are not immune to the trials and tribulations that come with helping others become well.

THE GIFT OF MIRACLES

A *miracle* is defined as "an effect or extraordinary event in the physical world that surpasses all known human or natural powers and is ascribed to a supernatural cause."[1] In essence, a miracle is a supernatural occurrence that defies all natural laws. The gift of miracles then, is God using you as a conduit to manifest the power of the Spirit, supernaturally defying natural laws. The result is a supernatural display of power that has some form of instantaneous result. For example, when a believer casts a demon out of an oppressed person and the unclean spirit comes out of that person, it produces an instantaneous supernatural result.

I'll never forget the first demon I was delivered from in December of 2000. When I understood God's word for what God's word says, I knew that I had a history of behaviors that I could not control, but they weren't totally gone. I equate those behaviors to a jack-in-the-box. When I turned my life completely over to God in 1998, I did not have near as many problems with my temper or moodiness; however, it always had the ability to pop up. I was real good at closing the lid on the anger-in-the-box of my body, but there were exterior forces that existed and that would turn that handle enough to cause the lid to pop open. The end result would be anger unleashed. When I learned that anger was the name of an unclean spirit, and it had a rank in satan's army, I knew that I had a demonic issue instead of a behavioral issue. The world will always attribute demonic issues to behavioral or hereditary issues because that is all they have been taught. Since the world doesn't know or trust in God's word, worldly people are ignorant to satan's devices.

When John the Baptist came preaching in the wilderness of Judea that Jesus was coming, he made an interesting statement. He said, *"And even now the ax is laid to the root of the trees. Therefore every tree which does not bear good fruit is cut down and thrown into the fire"* (Matt. 3:10). If you study the Bible, you will find that God uses many examples of trees to describe people. Though I'll leave that one to you, there are many scriptures you can find on this subject. The importance of this scripture lies in the word *ax*. John was foretelling that the ax would be laid to the root. This brings up two key questions:

- What does the ax represent?

- What does the root of the trees refer to?

The ax here represents Jesus—He is the ax. He is the one, and the only one, who has the ability to cut the root of any problems away. The root of the tree is the root of your problems. John is saying that Jesus is going to take the ax and cut the root of all your problems away. If you have an anger problem, Jesus can cut the root of anger.

Think about this concept for a moment: when you have shrubs outside of your home, those shrubs need to be trimmed back for maintenance in order for them to continue to look nice and presentable. As they grow back, the yardman comes back and trims the hedges to get them looking presentable again. This same concept holds true in counseling. Many psychiatrists and psychologists are "human hedge trimmers." When our problems get out of control, we go into the psychologist to get trimmed up and cleaned up so that we can be presentable in the public eye again. As always, our problems seem to manifest all around us again—we go back for another dose of counseling and medication to get all fixed up. The problem with this, just like with our shrubs, is that it is a never-ending maintenance issue. I am not attempting to throw all psychiatrists, psychologists, and counselors "under the bus"! There are those, who have a Christian worldview, who do a great job helping people through their problems. However, the analogy about hedge trimming is very accurate in describing many common counseling methods.

If you were to pull your shrubs up by the root, would you have to worry about your shrubs needing to be trimmed again? No! The root of the plant was removed, which ended the need for trimming. Jesus works in much the same way. When I cast the unclean spirit of anger out of myself, in the name of Jesus, in late 2000, the root of anger came out of me. The ax was laid to the root of my problem. Jack-in-the-box got ripped out of his house and thrown away. You see, the unclean spirit thought it had a house, and its roots were dug deep into the soil of my flesh. Although I could control its actions most of the time by putting a lid on it, that spirit always had the potential for growth. It always had potential to burst out of that box through the lid of my mouth. Now that the root of anger has been cut, I have not had to deal with anger issues of any kind in almost a decade! Praise God!

This does not mean I have been exempt from frustration or the temptation to get angry. Temptations will always be in front of us, but how we respond to those temptations is what makes all the difference. All anger is not sin, either. The Bible instructs us to be angry without sinning (see Eph. 4:26); therefore, there is a type of anger that is permissible at times. The thing one must understand is that if there is a consistent pattern of anger in someone's life, it is a demonic problem. The solution would lie in the blood of Jesus, not an anger management course. The manifestation gift of miracles can help change someone's life forever!

NOTE

1. "Miracle." Dictionary.com. Dictionary.com Unabridged. Random House, Inc. http://dictionary. reference.com/browse/miracle (accessed: March 18, 2012).

Chapter 16

PROPHECY

PROPHECY DEFINED

The gift of prophecy is also a manifestation of the Holy Spirit of God, speaking through an earthly vessel for divine instruction. The definition of prophecy is "the foretelling or prediction of what is to come."[1] It is also described as "something that is declared by a prophet, especially a divinely inspired prediction, instruction, or exhortation."[2] Prophecy truly is the foretelling of an event. In today's world, you can turn on the television and see a hundred different mediums foretelling futures and events. Prophecy, in its corrupted form, is all around us each and every day. On the other hand, true prophecy, in its purest form, is sometimes harder to come by. Therefore, people tend to be a little leery of it. Satan is very good, very loud, and very boisterous when it comes to perverting something of God's meant to be so pure and powerful. That's why you see so much junk on television and on the movie screen.

But one of the real messages here lies in the fact that, deep down, we all have a yearning to know more about supernatural things.

This is the very reason why movies concerning supernatural events are the top blockbusters at the box office. We are totally intrigued by the supernatural realm. As I write this book, in the last month, Americans have spent over $300 million at the box office on movies concerning the supernatural. In fact, 19 out of the top 25 grossing movies of all time are related to some kind of supernatural phenomenon, even if sometimes it is just the latest superhero movie, which always consists of supernatural powers. But if you examine your own life and the lives of those around you, you will find that the majority of movies you and your circle of friends have a keen interest in are centered on supernatural characters and events. This is also why people get drunk or use drugs—to launch themselves into another realm, hoping that it becomes supernatural.

If this holds true, why would people not be totally intrigued with prophecy? I have always said that if satan and all of his demons can display all the power that they do through movies, witchcraft books, witchcraft and warcraft games, toys, and so many other mediums, then how much power do you think the Lord God in heaven can demonstrate through His people? The answer is "A lot more!" God is the God of power. He is the power source and He is looking for willing vessels to display His power through.

Does He demonstrate His power on His own? Sure, He does, but He also loves to use His servants to display His power here on earth.

Much of the western church denies the power of God and, because of this, God doesn't bother those people with His power. God is looking for a willing spirit. In fact, the Bible says, *"For the eyes of the Lord run to and fro throughout the whole earth, to show Himself strong on behalf of those whose heart is loyal to Him"* (2 Chron. 16:9). Here is a three-point synopsis we can take from this scripture:

- God is watching the whole earth

- Searching for hearts who are after His

- To work mightily through them

PERSONAL PROPHECY

This is exactly why God still prophetically speaks through His servants. In general, there are two forms of prophecy: corporate and individual. I am going to address individual prophecy here, as it relates to you and the Holy Spirit. In personal prophecy, a person prophesying to you is ultimately going to give you glimpses of things that are coming your way in life.

Prophecy is meant to encourage you and build you up. The apostle Paul said, *"Pursue love, and desire spiritual gifts, but especially that you may prophesy"* (1 Cor. 14:1). And he went on to say, *"But he who prophesies edifies the church"* (1 Cor. 14:4). In other words, he who prophesies builds up people and encourages them, which essentially builds up the body of Christ since it is made of people. Prophecy and prophetic words, which are directed by the Holy Spirit of God, are crucial for the building up of the church. People need encouragement. They have a significant need to be built up while the world is trying to tear them down and cause them to doubt their dreams and destinies.

A PIECE OF THE PUZZLE

A prophecy will generally consist of three parts:

- It tells you where you have been—this gets your attention.

- It tells you where you are— this confirms to you that He knows you and you know it's Him.

- It tells you where you are going—this encourages you about His plans for you.

A person who operates with the spiritual gift of prophecy understands that we prophesy in part, as the Bible says, and on which Paul taught very well. God shows us things only in part, or partially. And God has us prophesy in part as well: *"For we know in part and we prophesy in part"* (1 Cor. 13:9).

Here is how good God is: He uses prophecy to give you glimpses of your future so that you continue to press on for the higher calling of Christ Jesus in your life. It's like a huge life-puzzle. God gives you a few pieces of the puzzle of what your future is supposed to be like, and seeing it gives you the faith to hold on in difficult times. When you can't see the whole picture, you know that God showed you some pieces to the puzzle that will fit right where they are supposed to be some day. You just have to keep fighting the good fight of faith and finish the puzzle. This is why God said through Jeremiah:

> For I know the thoughts that I think toward you, says the Lord, thoughts of peace and not of evil, to give you a future and a hope. Then you will call upon Me and go and pray to Me, and I will listen to you. And you will seek Me and find Me, when you search for Me with all your heart (Jeremiah 29:11-13).

If God gave us the whole prophecy up front and we knew every piece of the puzzle from the beginning, then we wouldn't need Him anymore. There would be no need to go and pray and seek Him. Prophecy keeps us built up, but it keeps us continually reliant upon Him to carry us through to our destiny in Christ. God needs more of His believers in today's world to eagerly desire the gift of prophecy. Paul wished that all of us would prophesy (see 1 Cor. 14:5). All, in the original Greek text, means "all"! All means the same yesterday, today, and probably forever! God wants to fill you with power from on high so that the Holy Spirit can speak through you. Are you willing?

PROPHECY IN ACTION

I remember a time when I was traveling on an airplane from Texas to Tennessee. I was sitting next to a young lady who seemed to be about 19-21 years old. As we were flying, and I was minding my own business, the Lord began to speak to me about this young lady. He began to show me a few things about her life, and He wanted me to encourage her. I do not believe she had a real relationship with the Lord.

So I began talking with her through casual conversation, which finally led me to a point where I could ask her a question. I remember asking her, "Was swinging your favorite thing to do as a little girl?"

Her eyes got really big as she perked up and asked, "Why did you ask that?"

I told her I could see when she was a little girl growing up in Florida, and I saw this apartment complex with a playground beside it, and all I could see was her continually swinging on the swings. This little word from the Lord really blew her away. She did not quite know what to think, but I had her full attention.

I told her about her present situation in life, and about the boyfriend she had. But the real meat of the story is what I told her about what God wanted to do in her life, and how He had a tremendous plan for her life. I believe I remember talking to her about choices, and that she was going to have to choose whether or not she was going to go with God. She got off the plane that day knowing that God knew where she had been. He validated to her that He knew exactly where she was and let her know that He was pulling on the strings of her heart to trust in Him, and follow Him all the days of her life. I honestly don't know what happened after that; but what I do know is that I could have not seen any of that stuff without the help of the Holy Spirit manifesting through me with the gift of prophecy.

NOTES

1. "Prophecy." Dictionary.com. Dictionary.com Unabridged. Random House, Inc. http://dictionary.reference.com/browse/prophecy (accessed: March 18, 2012).

2. Ibid.

Chapter 17

DISCERNING OF SPIRITS

DEFINING DISCERNMENT

The discerning of spirits is quite an interesting manifestation gift of the Holy Spirit. From the standpoint of personal observation, this particular gift is the most commonly used and recognizable gift for a person who has received the promise of the Holy Spirit. The reason for this lies in the area of being able to see with spiritual eyes. We have natural eyes, and we have corresponding spiritual eyes. Our physical eyes see physical things; however, people can become quite confused with what they see with their physical eyes because they can get hit with spiritual forces working against them in addition to the natural forces working against them.

Discernment is defined as "the faculty of discerning; discrimination; acuteness of judgment and understanding."[1] In spiritual terms, discernment is the ability to see "through" a situation. It is a spiritual understanding. It is not merely seeing or discerning with our eyes only, but we are able to spiritually discern things with all five of our senses. We can discern with our touch, with our sense of smell, and with our ears in what we hear with an acute spiritual ear. We can also discern with our mouth by taste, and with our eyes by what we see.

Upon receiving the promise of the Holy Spirit, I often tell people I have ministered to that they are just like a soldier, prepared for battle. Before receiving the power of the Spirit, they were already a soldier of Christ. They were saved and became a member of God's army—though they were not too well equipped. Now I tell them that it is as if they have gotten an infrared scope for the very first time, and are now being able to see the enemy in the darkness. If a soldier does not have infrared gear, he can only battle the enemy effectively in the light. God calls us to be the light, piercing through the darkness. It is pretty hard to win a battle in the darkness when your enemy can see in the dark but you can't. That's a perfect formula for getting killed. Praise God the Holy Spirit can see in the dark! Once we receive the promise of the Holy Spirit, He allows us to see things in this dark world that we used to be completely blind to.

DIFFERENT WAYS TO DISCERN

The benefit of the gift of discerning of spirits is to be able to identify evil spirits working in and around people's lives, as it affects us. You might have people in or around your life that you could not quite figure out why the relationship always had friction in it. Upon receiving the power of the Holy Spirit, you instantly see the problem—it is not your friend or relative. The problem is the spirit that is working through that friend or relative, and you can see it as clear as day now!

Now that you see it, the Holy Spirit is able to give you insights as to how to pray for that person and how to pray for that relationship. I will mention that we are to never pray prayers of manipulation or control over someone's life. We have to pray for the will of the Father to be done, not our own will, for someone's situation. God may want to do something totally different with that person's life than what you may have in mind. Because of this, it is our job to bless people as we pray for them. If what we have in mind goes against what God has in mind, that is called witchcraft, and it is very dangerous ground to tread on.

SMELLING SPIRITS

Have you ever been in a situation where you could literally smell evil? There are many people that tell stories of evil presences in their homes, and many of those accounts contain stories of rotten smells.

Just a few weeks before finalizing this book, I ministered at a church where I gave a testimony of a young man that was in the process of being healed from autism at the age of 14. At the end of the service, a young mom came to the front of the church and asked me to pray for her 3-year-old son who had been diagnosed with autism. As I prayed for her son and cast demons out of him that were responsible for the autism, I smelled a vile stench in the air as a result of his burps. The spirits were coming out of his mouth as he was burping them up. There were two ladies behind the young woman who were interceding, and they could smell the stench as well. It wasn't the little boy's fault. Those spirits stunk really bad because of the nature of their name, rank, and assignment on the boy's life.

Even as I finish this particular story, I received a praise report on Facebook today (the day of the final copy going to the publisher) from the young mom. She let me know that since that ministry night, about three weeks prior, her little boy has continued to burp and make weird noises out of his rear end that has never happened before. She is noticing even more positive changes in him, just as she noticed changes in him on the first night of prayer. This is another example of laying hands on the sick and the sick going through the process of recovery. When you have the ability to discern spirits, you can sometimes smell unclean spirits. The same principles hold true for hearing or tasting evil as well.

TINGLING SENSATIONS

I have discerned the spirit of witchcraft before by having a tingling sensation in my fingers. It was that discernment of spirits, through touch, that allowed me to know that witchcraft was in my presence.

I'll never forget the story of being at the Six Flags amusement park in Arlington, Texas, last year with my family. I saw a teenage boy walking behind his dad, and when I noticed him he was about 60 feet away from me. He did not see me at the time, but I instantly sensed an evil presence of satanic origin around him. He was not dressed in gothic clothes, nor was there anything that showed me that in the physical realm. He continued to walk in our direction as we were waiting in line for food. As he passed by our area, about 10 feet away, I glanced up toward him again and this time he was looking straight at me. As soon as I looked at him, he thrust his hand at me and made the sign of the devil right at me. It was a message that spoke louder than any words. It was his spirit speaking to my spirit, and his spirit was saying, "I don't care about your Jesus, nor do I care for whatever power you think you have. I serve satan, so take this and stick it right where the sun doesn't shine!"

That's how quickly the discernment of spirits operates. If I had not been walking in the power of the Holy Spirit, I would not have been able to see any evil associated with that boy whatsoever. Nor would that boy have cared one bit about my presence at Six Flags. He would have kept walking as normal because I did not do anything that would have provoked him to do what he did.

HOTEL SCARE

At another time, when we were on vacation, I was talking with a friend of mine out on the lawn of our hotel. He was really searching for some kind of significance in his life. He told me that there was something about me that was different than other people he knew, and that he knew what it was. He told me that it was God, and he said that he needed to get right with God. It started getting late, so we decided to walk back to the lobby and go to our rooms. As we rode the elevator, I asked him if he wanted to visit some more and get right with God. He said that he did, so we stopped on his floor and went to his room.

I took my shoes off, grabbed a chair, and we sat down and started visiting. My chair was in the back corner of the hotel room, and my friend was sitting on the end of the closest bed to me. As we talked about Jesus, he began to really dig deep in questioning if I was really serious about what I believed. My response was always a resounding, "Yes." As we continued to talk about Jesus and the power of Jesus Christ coming into his life, his eyes began to get extremely red. Snot started drooling out of his nostrils and his countenance turned very solemn. At this point I discerned that I was dealing with either a murderer, or someone who had been heavily involved in satanism. Since I had experience in ministering to other people who had prior involvements in satanic cults, I knew some of the characteristics of how that spirit operated.

Fortunately, I had to go to the restroom. So I took the liberty of using that as an excuse to get up. I was really uncomfortable with the situation even though I am not scared of the devil or his demons. I asked Jesus in the bathroom, "Lord, what do You want me to do?" There was no definitive answer.

I walked out of the bathroom and saw my friend standing up in between the two beds. I leaned up against the bathroom wall, and he slowly turned his head toward me and said, "You will remember this night forever!"

As soon as he said that, a supernatural force totally surrounded me. There is no doubt in my mind that it was an angel of God that literally wrapped its wings around me, and whispered very clearly in my ear: "Get out, now!" I reached down, grabbed my shoes, and I said, "I gotta go." And I left.

The next morning, I met with my friend again, but this time we stayed out in the light of day! I asked him about how he acted the night before, and he had no physical recollection of the things he said to me once he had begun to get red-eyed and snotty-nosed. I told him what happened, and he was not shocked. He began to confess to me why he wanted to have God in his life, but he did not feel like He would ever forgive him. At an earlier point in his life, he had been a member of a satanic cult and his role was to get girls pregnant for the sole purpose of using that baby as a human sacrifice. The devil had really lied to this guy, and the enemy had him almost totally convinced that he was going to own him forever, and that God would never accept him.

I had to tell him otherwise. He gave his life to the Lord that day, and I later baptized him in the river behind my house. I do not have a relationship with him today, but I do pray that he lives out his life as a Christian and does not turn back. He has seen the dark side at its darkest point, and he has also seen the light. The funny thing about this story is that he was reading a book about power when all of this was going on, which was not a Christian book. It was about how to become powerful and controlling. People are desperately looking to find power in their lives. We must help them find the power of God because it is the only true power that has order to it. All other sources of power will go out of control and fail.

BIBLICAL ILLUSTRATIONS OF DISCERNMENT

A clear biblical illustration of the gift of the discerning of spirits occurred when Jesus rebuked Peter after he tried to tell Him that He didn't have to suffer and die. Jesus replied, *"Get behind Me, Satan! You are an offense to Me, for you are not mindful of the things of God, but the things of men"* (Matt. 16:23). Jesus was not addressing Peter here, but He spoke directly to the spirit that was speaking through Peter's mouth.

Another illustration of the discerning of spirits occurred when Paul and Silas were ministering the gospel in Philippi. A slave girl kept following Paul around for days, proclaiming, *"These men are the servants of the Most High God, who proclaim to us the way of salvation"* (Acts 16:17). The Bible tells us that the girl had a spirit of divination and made her masters money by fortune-telling, but Paul had enough of her following them around and mocking them. He cast the spirit of divination out of her, thus ending her fortune-telling days. This made her masters mad because it took away their profits, so they were able to have Paul and Silas beaten with rods and thrown into prison. The enemy is always trying to launch an attack on you when you operate in the power of the Holy Spirit. Don't think for one second that you are not going to stir up some voices in hell over your valiant Christian efforts. That's part of the duty and responsibility of taking up your cross and following Jesus. Any good soldier of Christ will partake in trials, testings, and persecutions.

You are in the middle of a spiritual war, whether or not you have the discernment of spirits operating in your life. Paul reminds us:

Put on the whole armor of God, that you may be able to stand against the wiles of the devil. For we do not wrestle against flesh and blood, but against principalities, against powers, against the rulers of the darkness of this age, against spiritual hosts of wickedness in the heavenly places. Therefore take up the whole armor of God, that you may be able to withstand in the evil day, and having done all, to stand (Ephesians 6:11-13).

Not only do I want to put on the whole armor of God, but I also want the Holy Spirit to come upon me with power and fire, giving me the gift of discerning of spirits. I want to clearly see the enemy in front of me. Do you? It will require you to eagerly desire the promise of the Holy Spirit in and upon your life.

NOTE

1. "Discernment." Dictionary.com. Dictionary.com Unabridged. Random House, Inc. http://diction-ary.reference.com/browse/discernment (accessed: March 18, 2012).

Chapter 18

TONGUES AND INTERPRETATIONS

THE GIFT OF SPEAKING IN TONGUES

The eighth and ninth manifestation gifts of the Holy Spirit are different kinds of tongues and interpretation of tongues. Even though speaking in tongues is one gift, there are generally two types of tongues that will manifest by way of the Holy Spirit. First, there is the gift of tongues that involves praying to God in unknown languages. This is what many people call a "prayer language."

Paul said, *"For he who speaks in a tongue does not speak to men but to God, for no one understands him; however, in the spirit he speaks mysteries"* (1 Cor. 14:2). Paul then goes on to say many things about tongues in First Corinthians 14, which is incredible instruction for all believers. We would have a lot less arguments in the body of Christ if a lot of so called Spirit-filled believers would follow Paul's instructions, which, in reality, are instructions from God. The gift of tongues gets a bad reputation out in the church world because of television evangelists and Pentecostal preachers who use this gift loosely in their ministries.

For example, I have seen numerous "big name" preachers on television delivering a sermon across worldwide networks. During their message, they make a point, and then they start rattling off a few words in an unknown tongue before they go back to speaking English again. The sad thing is that some of these people are ministers who have national and international prominence! I would expect their spiritual maturity to be well beyond that—they must not be paying too much attention to what Paul says about tongues. They tend to discredit themselves with babbling for three to five seconds in tongues through the airwaves, and it goes without interpretation. This makes their prayer contradict scripture, and we wonder why so many Christians have a problem with people who speak in tongues. It is these people not acting mature enough in front of the church to handle themselves rightly before men.

Here are some of the reasons from Paul's teaching in First Corinthians 14 on why we are to pray in tongues directly to God, and not to man, when it is in reference to our personal prayers:

- No one understands you (see 1 Cor. 14:2).

- He who speaks in a tongue edifies himself (see 1 Cor. 14:4).

- There is no profit if I come speaking to you in tongues (see 1 Cor. 14:6).

- There is no point unless you utter by the tongue words easy to understand (see 1 Cor. 14:9).

- If I do not know the meaning of a language, I will be a foreigner to him who speaks, and he who speaks will be a foreigner to me (see 1 Cor. 14:11).

- In church, I would rather speak five words in my own language than 10,000 in a tongue (see 1 Cor. 14:19).

- If you speak in a tongue to unbelievers, they just think you are crazy (see 1 Cor. 14:23)—which happens too often in our world. When you are preaching on television, you have to understand that there are multitudes of people watching who don't know Jesus, tongues are irrelevant to them, and it turns them away from an otherwise anointed message.

In other words, the personal gift of tongues is a manifestation of the gift of the Holy Spirit of God that will allow you to utter mysteries to God. But God is not concerned about any of us trying to impress others with this newfound language we received. This language is special, and you should eagerly desire to speak in tongues, but it is still for you to pray to God by yourself. The Bible says that when we pray in tongues, we are building up ourselves: *"He who speaks in a tongue edifies himself…"* (1 Cor. 14:4).

Did you know that when you exercise you are building up your physical body? You are also positively affecting your soul, because your soul is made up of your mind, will, and emotions. Therefore, physical exercise greatly benefits the body and the soul. Speaking in tongues is analogous to physical exercise for the spirit. When you speak in tongues, you are literally building up your spirit and your soul. Your physical and spiritual states of being both affect your soul. However, the most important point for praying in tongues is uttering mysteries unto God and building up your spirit. We all need to build up our spirit!

What I like about praying in tongues is that it takes "me" out of the equation. When you pray mysteries to God, it is the Holy Spirit manifesting Himself through you! It is the Holy Spirit of God speaking straight to the Father through you! How incredible is that? You don't have to worry about selfish prayers, self-will, or anything of that nature. You are praying powerful, direct, focused, on target prayers to God! There is much fruit associated with praying in tongues consistently. This is why Paul said, *"I thank My God I speak with tongues more than you all"* (1 Cor. 14:18).

THE INTERPRETATION OF TONGUES

When tongues are spoken in the church, it should always be accompanied with an interpretation. This is where the ninth gift of the Spirit comes into operation. Paul reminded the Corinthians on this important subject:

Even so you, since you are zealous for spiritual gifts, let it be for the edification of the church that you seek to excel. Therefore let him who speaks in a tongue pray that he may interpret (1 Corinthians 14:12-13).

And he further went on to say:

If anyone speaks in a tongue, let there be two or at the most three, each in turn, and let one interpret. But if there is no interpreter, let him keep silent in church, and let him speak to himself and to God (1 Corinthians 14:27-28).

Here's a point-by-point breakdown of what all that means:

- Eagerly desire spiritual gifts, such as tongues.

- Let your motive be to build up the church.

- You can speak in a tongue in church, but there must be an interpretation.

- If there is no interpreter—do not pray in tongues in church—at all.

I certainly am not writing to beat up the church. I fear the Lord, and the last thing I want to do is bash the existing church. But I do believe that there are many out-of-control leaders in Pentecostal and

Charismatic circles who need to get a tighter grip on the scriptures. They are praying in tongues in their churches and on television without any interpretation, and they are doing it because that is what was modeled for them. Everything that is modeled to us is not always 100 percent accurate. We have to seek the heart of God and learn His word so that we don't become a stumbling block for lost people.

Overall, I want to encourage you to seek spiritual gifts. But first, you have to seek the Holy Spirit. He is the one who releases the gifts in and through us. It is important that we eagerly desire to prophesy and speak in tongues. As you do, you will become a stronger Christian and will become more effective in reaching lost souls. Be eager to become equipped with all that God has for you to fight the good fight of faith.

Chapter 19

OBEDIENCE BRINGS PROMISE

BAPTISM OF THE HOLY SPIRIT AND FIRE

At this point, there could be several questions running through your mind and heart. You may be thinking, "Although I am saved, what may be an indicator that I may not have received the power of the Holy Spirit yet, as described by John the Baptist and Jesus?"

Sometimes, there are Christians who really believe that they have received the promise of the Holy Spirit when they really haven't. Other times it is pride that keeps them from wanting to admit that they really don't walk with the power of the Holy Spirit present in their life. This relates to the attitude of, "I got everything I needed when I got saved." Whatever the reasons are, I believe there are some indicators that may be helpful to serve as signposts for whether or not the power of the Holy Spirit is operating in and around your Christian life.

Remember these words, "You will be baptized with the Holy Spirit and fire" (see Matt. 3:11).

Here are some indicators for you to go by:

- Have I healed the sick?

- Have I cleansed a leper?

- Have I raised the dead?

- Have I cast out a demon?

- Have I spoke in an unknown tongue?

- Have I prophesied over someone's life?

- Have I given a true word of knowledge to someone?

- Do I have the ability to discern spirits?

- Do I see extraordinary measures of faith in or around my ministry life?

- Do I see supernatural words of wisdom flow through me to others?

- Have I given interpretation of tongues?

- Am I reluctant to raise my hands in church while praising God?

In answering these questions, just use them as a gauge. I have yet to raise someone from the dead—but I have been baptized with the Holy Spirit and fire. These questions are a great way to get a feel for whether or not you and the Holy Spirit have had a real encounter. If none of these questions can relate to your life, it may be time for an encounter!

RECEIVE THE HOLY SPIRIT: OBEDIENCE

With all that you have read, I want to simplify the message so you have an understanding of how easily you can receive the promise of the Holy Spirit. First, I would like to cover a couple of conditions that are very important for you to understand—obedience and faith. I want to talk about obedience in this chapter and faith in the following one.

God, like any great father, loves for His children to obey Him. He has more wisdom and He has a better plan for your life. He can see farther for you than you can see for yourself. In fact, God says that He knew you before you were in your mother's womb (see Jer. 1:5)! His word declares, *"And we are His witnesses to these things, and so also is the Holy Spirit whom God has given to those who obey Him"* (Acts 5:32). And the Bible also says,

> *Beloved, if our heart does not condemn us, we have confidence toward God. And whatever we ask we receive from Him, because we keep His commandments and do those things that are pleasing in His sight* (1 John 3:21-22).

Having a desire to obey God in all that we do plays such a key role in having a trusting, intimate relationship with Him. It is very analogous to an earthly father and his child. If my sons are obedient, and if my sons strive to do things that are pleasing in my sight, then I have a desire to give them anything they ask for. Of course, all of this is done within reason. But God operates in a very similar way. He has principles, promises, rewards, and consequences in which He has laid out all throughout His word. He has rewards for obedience and He has consequences for disobedience presented very clearly to us throughout the Bible.

It is important to clearly understand that God doesn't just throw His Spirit around freely to every single person who asks of Him. Because God knows our hearts, He knows where we've been, where we are, and where we are going. It is up to us to have a heart of repentance, turning away from sin, and committed to obeying Him in all that we do. Will we fall short? Of course! God is not waiting for us to be perfect. He is just waiting on us to be obedient and to trust Him. That's why we need the power of the Holy Spirit so desperately.

Our human minds and wisdom cannot fight satan and his demonic armies on our own strength and with our own knowledge. If we are going to live a victorious Christian life here on earth, it will require being equipped with all of the tools that God has for us, so that we can do what Jesus came to do, which was to destroy the works of the devil (see 1 John 3:8)! Satan has been roaming the earth for thousands of years, and he knows all of the tricks in "the book." Consequently, we cannot match him with human wisdom and power. We need a power from on high! We need a supernatural force called the Holy Spirit to come upon each of us, and immerse us with power from heaven, so that we can combat the supernatural forces of evil upon this earth. Secondly, we need this supernatural power from on high so that we can be witnesses throughout the earth and see heaven filled with souls.

REPENTANCE

It is important to never forget that Peter walked with Jesus for three years as a believer! He had all the courage he ever needed as long as he was physically next to the Son of God; however, Peter had to fast and pray for ten days to receive what he needed to walk with that same boldness and courage after Jesus had left the earth. It is noteworthy to mention the fact that Peter had been disobedient by denying any relationship with Jesus upon His arrest in the Garden of Gethsemane. He lied! He also blasphemed God! However, if you read the last chapter of the Gospel of John, you will find that Peter had a repentant heart and Jesus forgave him for his acts of disobedience. If Peter needed this power from on high, how much more do we need it?

Therefore, the first key to receiving the promise of the Holy Spirit is to repent. All you have to do is pray and ask God to reveal to you any hidden sin or acts of disobedience that may hinder you from coming into a closer relationship with Him. Ask Him to convict you of anything that would hold you back from receiving all He has prepared for you and promised you. Then repent!

Sometimes, God will require you to confess a previously hidden sin to someone in whom you have sinned against. For example (I will use an extreme scenario here), let's say that a husband betrayed his wife and committed adultery some years ago. He has gotten his life right with God and repented. He asked for forgiveness and came clean with God. God already knew the whole situation anyway, but He forgives the man because he truly repented for his sin. As far as heaven is concerned, this man is now clean. If he died today, all signs point toward the fact that he will enter the kingdom of heaven for eternity. However, he does not die, and he has decades of life to live out his destiny in Christ Jesus. Because of this, God convicts the man in his heart to confess his prior sin to his wife. The Bible says to *"confess your trespasses to one another, and pray for one another, that you may be healed"* (James 5:16).

This man has a choice. He can keep his sin hidden and live in personal torment the rest of his life, or he can confess that sin to his wife and deal with the consequences. If he chooses to not confess what God had convicted him of, God may choose not to give him the promise of the Holy Spirit. But if he comes clean with his wife, his marriage has the possibility of becoming completely healed, and now there is nothing keeping him from receiving the power of the Holy Spirit. He doesn't have a disobedience issue to settle.

I have seen, through much experience, this parallel situation. God can forgive any human for any sin repented of and confessed to Him. But I have never seen a marriage capable of being fulfilled, healed, and sanctified (to be set apart and made holy), without hidden sin being brought out into the open. Otherwise, the devil and his demonic forces always have a playing card to deal with in that person's life.

The prior example was an extreme illustration, but there may be totally different scenarios. If you stole a lollipop from the convenience store when you were in 5th grade, I doubt if the Lord is requiring you to trace back those roots, find the convenience store owner, and pay him back. God may have convicted you or shown you that the stealing of the lollipop was wrong and you need to repent for the act of stealing. I believe this whole process merely requires an examination of the heart. The Bible promises, *"Draw near to God and He will draw near to you. Cleanse your hands, you sinners, and purify your hearts you double-minded"* (James 4:8).

The examples above are not biblical doctrine! They are merely examples of how God can deal with a person's heart in regards to unconfessed sin. The word of God is the only 100 percent truth in which we can be guaranteed of. I never attempt to put God in "a box," meaning that He is going to act a certain way, or respond a certain way, to a specific situation. This is why one must cry out to God and seek Him for direction concerning drawing closer to Him.

That's why God's word says "draw near unto Him and He will draw near unto you" (see James 4:8). This concept is really simple! As we draw near to God and speak to Him, He will draw near to us and speak to us—even in a sinful state! It is like an earthly father who loves his son, but who has not had a healthy relationship with him for years. His son has grown distant due to a few issues of disobedience and is feeling guilty about the whole mess, but he finally musters up enough courage one day to sit down with his dad and talk. He draws near to his dad in conversation, and his father begins to speak truth and love into his son's life. The wise father forgives his son, and tells him, in love, how he can make things right. The son now has a choice: to move forward or retreat back into the disobedience. If he moves forward in obedience, there will be blessing and reward. It's real simple.

Chapter 20

FAITH BRINGS PROMISE

THE CLARITY OF FAITH

The second key to receiving the Holy Spirit is faith! Faith is such a misused and misunderstood word that is used by multitudes of people. By definition, *"Faith is the substance of things hoped for, the evidence of things not seen"* (Heb. 11:1). In other words, faith is what makes up all of the energy that you gather and hold onto when you want something that you haven't put your hands on yet.

I'll never forget how badly I wanted my first Atari video game system when I was a freshman in high school. I put all of my energy into believing that I was going to get an Atari for Christmas. I told everybody I was going to get an Atari, and all of my thoughts and actions for over a month were centered on looking under the tree on December 25th and seeing an Atari video game system right before my eyes. My parents did not have the extra money to buy a gift like that for me; and I was even told by them that they could not afford an Atari system. Although all of the exterior forces around me in the natural, ranging from words to facts, portrayed a picture of gloom and despair, I could still see that Atari gaming system under the tree. I was putting all of my energy and all of my focus into that and, on Christmas Day, my Atari video game system appeared under the tree! My grandmother came through, and I think my parents bought some games to go with it!

When we make big decisions in life, we don't always have 100 percent clarity and 100 percent of the answers that cause us to move forward with a decision. In fact, with most decisions you and I make, we only have about 80 percent clarity at the point of decision. The other 20 percent is our faith that gets involved. If we could go through life accumulating 100 percent certainty before moving forward with any decisions, life would be very easy, and hence, we would become our own god.

ABRAHAM AND SARAH

Faith is a wonderful thing! It is faith that led you to Christ. The Bible says, *"For by grace you have been saved through faith…"* (Eph. 2:8). It is the substance of a life hoped for, and evidence of that eternal life not seen! It will be by faith that you receive the power of the Holy Spirit as well. This is why the Bible says that *"without faith, it is impossible to please* [God]*"* (Heb. 11:6).

It was by faith that Abraham walked with God. *"By faith Abraham, when he was tested, offered up Isaac, and he who had received the promises offered up his only begotten son, of whom it was said, 'In Isaac your seed shall be called'"* (Heb. 11:17). Think about this situation for a moment: here is Abraham, whom God had promised that his descendants would be as many as the stars that he could see in the sky, yet he was 86 years old and Sarah was 85, and not to mention barren, when this promise came!

There is so much to be learned about faith through the story of Abraham and Sarah. Because they were people, like you and me, they had the same tendency to doubt the promises of God. One of the biggest lessons concerning faith is that God handles the time frames. The point of faith is to know that God will fulfill all He has spoken, revealed, or promised! In the case of Abraham and Sarah (known as Abram and Sarai at the time), all they could see was that Sarah was getting too advanced in age to bear children, so they decided that the promise that God had made was to come by another means. That's when, in their carnal minds, they determined that the only way they would produce an heir was through Sarai's maidservant Hagar.

Sometimes, if our answer to God's promise does not come in the time frame in which we think it should fall in, or in the method of delivery that we think it should have come, then we discount the very promises of God. This can lead to a severe drought in our lives, otherwise known as a "wilderness experience"! God will allow us to walk through a wilderness experience so that we become more reliant on Him, on His voice and direction. Sometimes we can delay God's promises to us in our own lives because we interfere with the methods of God's packaging and delivery systems. The Bible again reminds us,

> *"For My thoughts are not your thoughts, nor are your ways My ways," says the Lord. "For as the heavens are higher than the earth, so are My ways higher than your ways, and my thoughts than your thoughts"* (Isaiah 55:8-9).

At this point, God had already promised Abram that his descendants would be as vast as the stars; however, he and Sarai decided to fulfill this promise by their own means, which we do so often.

Here's the basic outline of this story, accompanied by the situations and circumstances described:

Abram received a huge promise from God when he was 86 years old. It didn't seem possible.

Sarai, his wife, was 85 years old and barren—this also doesn't seem possible in the natural.

So Abram and Sarai try to put the "pieces of the puzzle" together and come up with a solution. "We do things in our own strength based on the knowledge that we have," which is often what we do as well.

Their solution is for Abram to marry Sarai's maid-servant, Hagar, and bear an heir to the promise through her. This is seen as fixing the problem yourself and getting ahead of God.

So Hagar bears Abram a son, whom they name Ishmael. There are consequences for all actions.

God allows 13 years go by and revisits Abram on the issue of His promise to him. This took a long time, sometimes like the wilderness experiences of our own lives. But God did come back for Him to fulfill His promise.

Ishmael was 13 years old, but still not the child of the initial promise—God still loves all of us as demonstrated through His affection for Ishmael and Hagar after being sent away.

It is at this point that God changes Abram and Sarai's names to Abraham and Sarah. This signifies the destiny God always had for them; and can now be seen as a reflection of our own lives as the great plan He has for us because of His love for us.

God reminds Abraham that Sarah will have a son—demonstrating the need for prophecy today.

But when Sarah overhears the conversation outside the tent, she laughs at God. She expresses hope without faith.

God said, *"Is anything too hard for the Lord? At the appointed time I will return to you, according to the time of life, and Sarah will have a son"* (Gen. 18:14). And Jesus said, "I will send the Helper" (see John 15:26). We are to trust in Him and lean not on own understanding.

So, at the age of 99 years old, Sarah gave birth to the child of God's promise, which was given to Abraham 14 years before. God will fulfill all that He speaks; this can be even through prophecy today.

His name was Isaac, in whom we are descendants of! *"In Isaac your seed shall be called"* (Heb. 11:18). God always fulfills His promises. This is even carried over into the promise of us receiving the Holy Spirit and power (see Acts 1:8).

FAITH PLAYS A CRUCIAL ROLE

The message in all of this is that our faith plays such a crucial role in receiving all that God has promised us in His word. The Bible says that *"faith comes by hearing, and hearing by the word of God"* (Rom. 10:17). Abraham heard the word of the Lord, yet he did not have the faith to hold onto the promise until he heard more of the word of the Lord.

As we continue to "hear" the word of God, our faith continues to develop. Faith comes by "hearing," and "hearing" by the word of God. Where people have failed in the past and not received the promise of the Holy Spirit is when they heard the word of God as it relates to receiving Holy Spirit power, and they submit to being prayed for to receive the power of the Holy Spirit, then if they did not get immersed with power from on high immediately, they begin to question God's word and lose the faith necessary to fulfill the promise of God's word and His plan for their life. Just like Abraham, we tend to devise our own plan to justify God's word, when God's plans were for us to simply keep hearing His word and developing our faith.

After the birth of Isaac, Abraham had matured in his faith to the point where he was diligent about "hearing" the word of the Lord and developing his faith. When Abraham was instructed to take Isaac up to the land of Moriah and sacrifice him on one of the mountains, he acted on faith. But he did not quit hearing! Even when Isaac helped his father, and noticed that they had wood, fire, and a knife, but no lamb, he asked his father,

"Look, the fire and the wood, but where is the lamb for the burnt offering?"

And Abraham said, "My son, God will pro-vide for Himself the lamb for a burnt offering" (Genesis 22:7-8).

Abraham was remaining strong in his faith, amidst the picture of his current situation. God had made a promise to him that his seed would multiply to the ends of the earth, even though things were looking pretty grim.

As the story unfolds, Abraham laid his son on the altar to offer him up as a sacrifice to the Lord by faith. However, as Abraham stretched out his hand with his knife, in order to sacrifice Isaac, and angel of the Lord called to Abraham from heaven, "Abraham, Abraham!"

So Abraham said, "Here I am." Praise God that Abraham had continued to hear! Faith comes by hearing, and hearing by the word of God (see Rom. 10:17). Because Abraham had heard and continued to hear, he had tremendous faith in God, knowing that He will deliver on all of His promises to His children. The angel instructed Abraham to not lay a hand on Isaac, for he had shown God that he feared Him greatly and was willing to do whatever God asked of him.

Faith is the pure substance of holding onto what God has promised us in His word, not what someone has misinterpreted to us from God's word. Your faith can be developed by consistently feasting on God's word. If God says, *"For the promise* (of the Holy Spirit) *is to you and your children, and to all who are afar off, as many as the Lord our God will call"* (Acts 2:39), then you have to ask yourself a couple of questions. First, are you a child of the promise? Are you truly a son of Abraham, Isaac, and Jacob? Secondly, has the Lord our God called you? If your answer is yes to these questions, then the promise of the Holy Spirit, as described in the Book of Acts, is for you just like the Holy Spirit was available to Peter.

Chapter 21

HOLD FAST AND HUNGER

WE NEED THE HOLY SPIRIT

You and I need the Holy Spirit as badly as Peter did, because neither you nor I ever had a chance to walk around with Jesus for three years, twenty-four hours a day, seven days a week! This may require you, like it did Sarah, to step out of your comfort zone on theological beliefs and trust God's word. This may require you to dig in and press in toward God, crying out to Him for all He has for you. This may require for you to pray and fast, to seek God for His promises to you and your children.

A great reminder is that the first disciples of Jesus had to pray and fast for ten days to receive the promise of the Holy Spirit. It strikes me as odd when someone doesn't get their answer in two seconds, how they turn to discounting the minister and the message. Ultimately, they discount God's word and His promises.

The apostle James, in his book, wrote to the church on the issue of faith and, in particular, the development of faith. In chapter 1 of his book, he writes:

If any of you lacks wisdom, let him ask of God, who gives to all liberally and without reproach, and it will be given to him. But let him ask in faith, with no doubting, for he who doubts is like a wave of the sea driven and tossed by the wind. For let not that man suppose that he will receive anything from the Lord; he is a double-minded man, unstable in all his ways (James 1:5-8).

Whether we are asking for wisdom or anything else in our Christian walk, we must ask in faith without doubting. I can picture James as if he were preaching this at every large church gathering throughout Asia, and I can see him shaking his finger at the people saying, "Make sure that those people know that they will not receive any answers to their prayers because of their doubting ways! They are unstable, and they have no faith. Don't you know that faith comes by hearing, and hearing by the word of God? Hear the word of God and develop your faith! Trust in Him, and He will answer you!

"Our fathers taught us to trust in Him and lean not on our own understanding, and in all our ways acknowledge Him, and He will direct our paths. Don't you know that He is able to do exceedingly and abundantly more than anything we ask of Him?

So, ask in faith and hold steadfast! Call unto Him, and He will show you great and mighty things in which you do not know! Don't you know that if a child asks his father for bread, why would he give him a stone? Or if he asks his father for an egg, why would he give him a scorpion? So, if you being evil give good gifts to your children, how much more will your Father in heaven give the Holy Spirit to those who ask Him?

"So, my faithful brethren, just because your Atari doesn't show up under the tree on December 23rd, it doesn't mean that the Atari won't be under the tree as promised on December 25th. Just have faith, and trust in the words of your Father! Don't be a doubter and get tossed to and fro by the winds of the sea all of your life. You need to act in faith. You need to live by faith. You need to speak in faith. You need to pray in faith. You need to receive the Holy Spirit by faith! If you don't have your answer in your time, keep hearing the word of the Lord and keep on believing that He is able, because nothing is too hard for the Lord! He will deliver the package if you trust in Him!"

FINAL WORDS OF ENCOURAGEMENT

I want to give you some final words of encouragement as you seek the promise of the Holy Spirit for your life. I have read many books about the Holy Spirit, but I don't always see that every roadblock is removed before one is given a model prayer to pray. The prayers are always good because receiving the

Holy Spirit can be as simple as asking God, but I want to help you make sure that you know that all stumbling blocks to you receiving God's best are removed.

This is not a formula! These are only guidelines for you to follow:

- Repent of any hidden sins.

- If you have ever made fun of or mocked an anointed minister of God, ask God to show you so that you can repent for it.

- If you have ever made fun of or mocked the gifts of the Spirit or the promise of the Holy Spirit, you will want to specifically repent for that as well.

- Ask God to cleanse you of all unrighteousness.

- Tell God that you believe His word.

- Tell God that you believe His promises are for you, and that you will receive them.

- Ask God to equip you with everything you need, according to His will.

- Tell God that you want to speak mysteries directly to Him by speaking in tongues.

- Tell Him that you want to be used as a vessel of honor by allowing His spiritual gifts to manifest through you.

- Fast if you feel like the Lord is convicting you to fast.

- Commit to pray and seek God for the Holy Spirit, whether it takes one second or ten years.

- When the time comes, lift up your arms to God and reach out to Him.

- When the time comes, open your mouth so that there are no restrictions.

- When the time comes, tell God that you want to receive the Holy Spirit in the name of Jesus.

- When the time comes, you may want to find an anointed minister of God to pray for you.

- When the time comes, you may be in your own closet or out in the woods. Don't limit when and where God is going to immerse you with the promise of the Holy Spirit.

Now it is time to dig in and hunger for God's best. This is your time! You have read the good news, and it is for you! God wants what is best for you, and He wants to equip you with the necessary spiritual giftings to fulfill the destiny He has prepared for you on this earth. It is time to embrace your destiny. Jesus said, *"Blessed are those who hunger and thirst for righteousness, for they shall be filled"* (Matt. 5:6).

Why not you? If not now, when? I pray that you receive God's best, and I pray that you "only believe!" So…it's time to start praying and holding fast to His promises.

PRAYER FOR THE PROMISE OF THE HOLY SPIRIT

Here is a sample prayer you may find helpful as you pursue the promise of the Holy Spirit:

Lord God, I am a child of Yours and I love You. I have repented for my sins, and I come to You now, to reach out to You and receive all the promises You have for me, according to Your word.

Your word says, "If you then, being evil, know how to give good gifts to your children, how much more will your heavenly Father give the Holy Spirit to those who ask of Him" (Luke 11:13).

Father, in the name of Jesus, I am asking You for the promise of the Holy Spirit. I am going to open my mouth and thirst. I am going to extend my arms to You. I am going to fix my eyes upon You. Please immerse me with power from heaven. Come upon me with power and fire, and fill me up with Your Spirit, the Holy Spirit. By faith, I receive You, more of You, in Jesus's name. Thank You, Father.

ABOUT DANNY MCDANIEL

Danny McDaniel is an entrepreneur and transformational speaker. He is also a co-founder and associate pastor of Bethel Dallas, a church in the DFW area. He has an extensive background in coaching high school football and track. Danny has a passion for developing leaders in our society, especially for equipping the next generation of leaders in our country. Above all, he is dedicated to being the best husband and father that he can be, raising up 3 young men that will change the world in which we live. He and his wife, Diane, are strong proponents of strengthening marital and family unity; and teaching parents how to raise kids who will serve God faithfully throughout their lives. Danny's oldest son, Cam is currently a sophomore football player at Notre Dame. Gavin is a junior in high school, and TJ is a 6th grader.

FOR MORE INFORMATION

The Champion Center

2680 MacArthur Blvd.
Lewisville, TX 75067

(972) 315-8668

www.DannyMcDaniel.com